World Music: A Very Short Introduction

VERY SHORT INTRODUCTIONS are for anyone wanting a stimulating and accessible way in to a new subject. They are written by experts, and have been published in 25 languages worldwide.

The series began in 1995, and now represents a wide variety of topics in history, philosophy, religion, science, and the humanities. Over the next few years it will grow to a library of around 200 volumes – a Very Short Introduction to everything from ancient Egypt and Indian philosophy to conceptual art and cosmology.

Very Short Introductions available now:

Available soon:

For more information visit our web site

www.oup.co.uk/vsi

Philip V. Bohlman

WORLD MUSIC

A Very Short Introduction

OXFORD
UNIVERSITY PRESS

OXFORD
UNIVERSITY PRESS

Great Clarendon Street, Oxford OX2 6DP

Oxford University Press is a department of the University of Oxford.
It furthers the University's objective of excellence in research, scholarship,
and education by publishing worldwide in

Oxford New York

Auckland Bangkok Buenos Aires Cape Town Chennai
Dar es Salaam Delhi Hong Kong Istanbul Karachi Kolkata
Kuala Lumpur Madrid Melbourne Mexico City Mumbai Nairobi
São Paulo Shanghai Singapore Taipei Tokyo Toronto

with an associated company in Berlin

Oxford is a registered trade mark of Oxford University Press
in the UK and in certain other countries

Published in the United States
by Oxford University Press Inc., New York

British Library Cataloguing in Publication Data
Data available

Library of Congress Cataloging in Publication Data
Data available

ISBN 0-19-285429-1

1 3 5 7 9 10 8 6 4 2

Typeset by RefineCatch Ltd, Bungay, Suffolk
Printed in Spain by Book Print S. L., Barcelona

For my students,
who have taught me more than they can imagine.

Contents

Preface

At the beginning of the 21st century it is impossible to define world music without slipping down a tautological slope. World music is that music we encounter, well, everywhere in the world. World music can be folk music, art music, or popular music; its practitioners may be amateur or professional. World music may be sacred, secular, or commercial; its performers may emphasize authenticity, while at the same time relying heavily on mediation to disseminate it to as many markets as possible. World music's consumers may use it as they please; they may celebrate it as their own or revel in its strangeness. The old definitions and distinctions don't hold anymore; world music can be Western or non-Western, acoustic or electronically mixed. The world of world music has no boundaries, therefore access to world music is open to all. There's ample justification to call just about anything world music.

World music is inseparable from another equally difficult to define phenomenon of our age, globalization. By the end of the year 2001, above all in the wake of the events of September 11th, it was no longer possible to deny the impact of globalization even on local, on-the-street realities. It remains hard to pin down, much less define, but few have failed to recognize the paradox in the rhetoric and reality of globalization. It's both good and bad, a worldview to be celebrated and vilified, a force that can contain the world but also a movement that must be contained by force. It could be said that globalization has two meanings, or indeed that it opens up two ways of encountering the world, and most people ally themselves with one or the other.

The two meanings of globalization are emblematic of the two contradictory ways in which 'world music' is understood today. In the course of this book I rely on both meanings for my own examination of what world music is today, paradoxes and all. For many, world music represents much that is right in the world, indeed, the very possibility that music and music-making bring people together. The sheer volume of world music – on the radio, CDs, and the Internet, and in university classrooms and books with diverse readerships – has never been greater. When it comes to celebrating globalization, world music is always within earshot.

There's also the darker side to world music. World music can raise fears that we are losing much that is close to home. Its homogenizing effect threatens village practices as it privileges the spaces of the global village. Its dissemination across the globe depends on the appropriation of transnational recording companies, whose primary interests are to exploit cultural resources. Fusion and border-crossing may enrich some world-music styles, but they impoverish others. At the beginning of the 21st century, there is much about the rhetoric and reality of globalization that has given world music a bad name.

In this book I seek a middle ground. I urge the reader both to look critically at the ways in which musicians and managers have turned to world music to appropriate and exploit traditional music and to recognize how the abundance of world music today offers the opportunity to experience the diversity of human societies like never before. The middle ground I seek does not avoid the dual meanings evident in the rhetoric of globalization or the discourse of world music, but rather it endeavours to represent the space of encounter, which is also the space in which the history of world music has unfolded. Accordingly, the middle ground in this book also affords me the opportunity to wrestle with the dilemma faced by all authors of these

'Very Short Introductions': dealing with a vast topic in a deliberately restricted space.

If there were a moment when globalization became truly globalized, it would appear to be the summer and autumn of 2001, during which time I completed the final revisions of this book. The rhetoric of globalization has reached new heights, and the word itself has become a household term. In the academic world, it has come of age as high theory, and few disciplines have managed to avoid its seductiveness at some level. Unquestionably, the key word on the 2001 conference circuit was globalization: on 18–19 May 2001, for example, my own university hosted an event it called the 'Third Annual Globalization Conference'. Globalization had seemingly won the day, providing theory and discourse for scholars of various stripes and from throughout the world, so that they could tackle the big issues of modern times.

More striking to the average residents of the global community was the extent to which the rhetoric of globalization mobilized many fellow residents to action. During the summer of 2001 the debates over globalization quite literally spilled onto the streets, notably at the mid-July 'G8 Summit', an event that brought together the representatives of a collective customarily designated as the 'world's seven wealthiest nations plus Russia'. In 2001, the summit convened in Genoa, Italy, where it was greeted by tens of thousands of protesters, who represented a broad range of political agendas, all now subsumed under the rubric 'anti-globalization'. In every imaginable permutation, the rhetoric of globalization fragmented into countless buzzwords. There was talk of 'global trade agreements' and 'global warming', 'global markets' and the 'global economy'. The rhetoric, nonetheless, was powerless when it came to stemming the problems at hand, the local problems that erupted when the anti-globalists rioted in the streets, clashed with the police mustered to defend the cause of globalization, and slid into a conflict that produced destruction, injury, and death.

In the aftermath of the events of September 11th, the rhetoric of globalization entered a radically new phase. The attacks themselves were directed toward 'symbols' of globalization, the World Trade Center and the Pentagon. The perpetrators were members of 'global terror networks', and stemming their spread required that a 'global alliance against terror' be mustered. World culture and world history were at stake, thus making it necessary to fight the war on terrorism on a 'global scale'. The rhetoric of globalization spread, but the possibilities of what it might really mean also multiplied. Many more people in the world imagined they felt the presence of globalization more directly in their own lives, but few were any closer to knowing whether it was something that brought comfort or that had the potential to destabilize the world as they knew it.

The unchecked proliferation of perspectives on globalization in 2001 also shed light on the vastly different meanings of world music. The term world music is itself relatively new, let's say two decades old. Prior to the early 1980s, all-encompassing terms to describe the musics of the world were rare, with preference given to regional categories or designations of genres; one studied and wrote about 'African music' or 'folk music', not world music. In the 1980s, the field of ethnomusicology took a turn toward what we might call big issues, approaching them comparatively and with more consciously interdisciplinary methods, and it followed that world music, for example in Bruno Nettl's highly influential writing, commanded greater attention. It was also during the 1980s that world music found its way into college and university music curricula, again as the result of a perceived need to study all the world's musics. Initially an alternative to 'Western art music', world music embraced more and more areas in the academic music curriculum, inspiring widespread rethinking of how music itself was to be taught.

World music is also that phenomenon that greets one on the new floors of large record shops, or in the 'international' bins of the CD sections in book shops. This is the world music that is omnipresent whenever we step into chain coffee shops, several of which market their own world-music CD blends next to their global coffee blends. In a word, this world music is traditional music repackaged and marketed as popular music. This world music, too, owes its origins to the 1980s, when the executives of record companies and advertising specialists determined that popular music from outside the Anglo-American and European mainstreams needed a distinctive name. During the 1980s, the record industry toyed with a few other names – worldbeat, world fusion, ethnopop, even tribal and new age – but by the 1990s, it was world music that enjoyed by far the greatest currency. Again, it was an issue of the truly global implications of the name itself. Maybe this kind of world music really was limited to the appropriation of traditional music as popular music, but its claims to globalization were surely well founded.

Given this preoccupation with the global signalled by the several meanings of 'world', one understands perfectly well why there is a tendency when approaching a subject as seemingly boundless as 'world music' to try to capture some measure of its vastness and variety. The wonder of it all, one might imagine, should ultimately entice and seduce the reader. There is an equally strong countertendency, however, that urges one to find something singular and unitary about a global phenomenon, thus to condense it and make it manageable for the reader. It is my goal in this Very Short Introduction to strike a balance between these two approaches. On one hand, I write as an ethnomusicologist, therefore world music is for me all the musics of the world. With that approach in mind, I have written this book so that it might give readers some sense of difference and might encourage them to ask why humans use music in so many ways: What does world music tell us about the diversity of human cultures? On the other hand, world music at the beginning of the 21st century has all the trappings of globalization, whose theorists endeavour to explain why cultural phenomena have increasingly come to demonstrate similarity. World music has long been mustered by both camps to provide evidence for new theories, whether they stress cultural relativism or universalism. Neither way of imagining world music is wrong; neither tells the whole story. For these reasons, this introduction attempts to negotiate the space between what world musics really are and what they are imagined to be.

Before readers get the feeling that I am equivocating about what world music is – simply acquiescing to the validity of all possible meanings – it is only fair for me to reveal some of the meanings world music has for me, meanings that have shaped the way I approach it in this book. World music is very much a construct of modernity, which is to say the encounter with and interpretation of the world that was unleashed by the Age of Discovery, the Enlightenment, colonial expansion, and the rise of the nation-state. Asserting that there is music everywhere in the world is, therefore, a Western concept, if it is also, however, a concept that results from Western encounters with the world. 'Encounter' is a crucial concept throughout the book. Encounters mark important historical moments; encounters bring about change, even revolution; encounters create the conditions for exchange. Cultural encounter itself is by no means Western; nonetheless, the growing sense in the past 500 years that encounter is not isolated but rather has ramifications for world history is.

At the beginning of the 21st century, then, world music is not simply the music of an exotic 'other'. Our encounters with the world have become quotidian, and music mediates those encounters, whether we perceive that or not. It is not simply a matter that television advertisement regularly draws on South Asian and West African drumming; it is not the weaving of world-music tracks into film soundtracks; it is not only the fact that Protestant hymnals are increasingly multicultural or that the Catholic Mass is musically familiar to every ethnic community in the metropolis; nor is it that Sufism has become a world religion mediated by world music; it does not even stop with the legal cases about musical ownership or the limits of downloading music from the Internet. It is, rather, the confluence of all these phenomena, which too must be understood as encounters that are imagined and mediated by the West. World music is an inescapable everyday experience, whether or not we understand what it means. In this Very Short Introduction I strongly make the case that there is much to be gained from understanding what it does mean.

This book unfolds as a series of thematic leitmotifs, each one assuming the form of a chapter. Though the chapter-length leitmotifs differ, the ways in which they are treated are similar, thereby making it possible to strive toward a certain degree of coverage while admitting to its limitations. All chapters employ the same structure, in other words, the same six sections through which I pursue the leitmotif of the different chapters. Each chapter begins with an encounter, and it proceeds through a series of historical, theoretical, and aesthetic sections via vignettes of musicians and scholars before arriving at popular music and the present. Within each chapter, therefore, I strive for internal consistency, returning in subsequent chapters to a point of beginning so that each chapter might become a narrative of encounter for the reader. The schema below summarizes the organizational structure of each chapter:

  i: Encounter with world music
  ii: Historical or theoretical excursus
 iii: Profile of a musician
 iv: Aesthetic issue, especially an examination of meaning and identity
  v: Profile of an ethnomusicologist or group of world-music scholars
 vi: Ethnographic present and popular music

Many of the encounters that fill the book are my own, in one way or another. They may come, more or less directly, from my own fieldwork; they may represent, rather more indirectly, musical practices that I have experienced through theoretical engagement, for example my special concern with the relation between religion and music; they may also arise from my own attempts to forge an approach that would enable me and, I hope, others to understand something of the whole of world music. This approach, then, is meant to encourage the reader to engage more directly with world music as *experience*.

It should not go without saying that the chapter organization I have employed for this book helps me deal with the problem of representative or equal coverage of all the world's music. Few readers will fail to notice rather quickly that all world musics do not make it into the book; they will also recognize that I return rather frequently to some parts of the world and to some repertories of music, whereas others receive more fleeting visits. In fact, I feel no need to make excuses or offer disclaimers for the music that is *not* in this book. Tokenism does not solve the problem of representative coverage, but rather exacerbates it, all the more so in a short introduction. More to the point, I understand many of the sections in the book as points of departure, or rather as invitations to readers who might wish to turn first encounters into excursions and experiences of their own. At the beginning of the 21st century, our everyday encounters with world music make this eminently possible.

This book was not initially my idea but that of George Miller, who stewards the Very Short Introductions through Oxford University Press. George put his faith in my ability to carry out the project, and I hope he recognizes in the end result even a small measure of my deep appreciation. I was especially fortunate that four very different readers – a current university music student; a former PhD student at the University of Chicago, now teaching ethnomusicology at the National Cheng-kung University in Taiwan; a trusted colleague at Chicago; and a distinguished pedagogue at the Open University in the UK – were willing to offer comments and suggestions on the final version of the manuscript: very special thanks for their time and insights go to Andrea Bohlman, Pi-yen Chen, Martin Stokes, and Martin Clayton. In writing a book on world music, one constantly realizes the ways communities and collectives shape what music means, locally and globally. Over the course of many years my students have constituted an especially meaningful collective, shaping my thinking about world music again and again. As a symbol of my appreciation for what my students have done for me, I am especially pleased to dedicate this book to them.

As always, the final word of acknowledgement goes to Andrea, Ben, and Christine, a marvellous collective of world and world-class musicians if there ever was one. Thanks for being there as we encountered world music at home and abroad, at border-crossings and on concert stages, wherever and whenever we seized the opportunity.

Philip V. Bohlman

List of illustrations

Maps

Chapter 1
In the beginning . . . myth and meaning in world music

First encounters

First encounters with world music happen in many different ways. Some of us travel great distances to encounter music quite unlike anything we know from our home. Others first become aware of world music close to home, perhaps because of a noticeable change in the familiar, perhaps through an epiphany that the familiar was not what we had imagined it to be. For still others, first encounters are through recordings, videos, or sundry forms of representation that at once draw attention to the distance between home and away, and possess the power to close that gap. The whole of world music may come into view because of an ability to focus on and perceive one meaningful part. First encounters, therefore, also connect parts to wholes. First encounters with world music are often personal, even intimate experiences, frequently engendering a sudden awareness of local knowledge. That awareness seldom leaves us untouched, rather it transforms us, often deeply. In our different ways we may greet world music with awe and wonderment, fear and reverence; we may marvel at the beauty of its simplicity or the cacophony produced by its complexity; we may find ourselves lost in a search for meanings not immediately apparent or transformed through unexpected revelation. However and wherever first encounters take place, they profoundly change what we perceive music to be and how we understand its functions and meanings in the lives of human beings. First encounters with world music are never isolated, passing events.

First encounters are the stuff of story and history, thus they are of great interest for us in this book. Myth is full of tales of first encounters. Just as myths tell about the intersections between the natural and the supernatural, or between humans and deities, so too do they tell about how music emerges at the points of intersection. In myths supernatural beings often confer music upon humans as a gift. The gift may be abstract, a component of perception or communication, say, of language. It might also be concrete, for example in the forging of musical instruments from physical objects, such as human or animal bodies, which thereby acquire metaphysical meaning. Where music originates differs more in degree than kind in the myths of the world's religions. Music may be evident in the songs of birds or communications from gods, or it may simply be 'out there' in the music of the spheres. It is as if music awaits encounter, the transcendence of humans through perception and representation of a divine order encoded by music. Tales about the origins of music have a virtually universal presence in religions throughout the world, suggesting that mythological encounters may be among the first conditions of world music.

We also weave the stories about first encounters into the grand narratives that form our histories of world music. Let's turn briefly to one of the earliest of these stories. The first encounter between the musics of old and new worlds took place in 1557, during the sojourn of a Huguenot missionary, Jean de Léry, among the Tupinamba at what is today – that is, long after the first encounters – known as the Bay of Rio de Janeiro. In a 1578 account, Léry wrote extensively about the music of the Tupinamba, even including transcriptions of melodies and texts used in specific rituals and with descriptions fleshing out the contexts of those rituals. Léry did not travel to the New World to write dispassionate, ethnographic observations, but rather to evangelize and convert, and his account therefore contains observations motivated by missionary zeal. The Tupinamba were cannibals, and the customs that accompanied the consumption of their fellow human beings understandably caught Léry's attention. They also caught the attention of other writers of the day, not least among them Montaigne, whose 'On Cannibals', largely a series of reflections on Léry's writings, nonetheless led to wide dissemination of Léry's description of the first encounter. Léry's writings on Tupinamba music and their reception, then, set a tradition of writing about world music in motion, a tradition that would accelerate through the Age of Discovery and the Early Modern era, culminating in Herder's late 18th-century collection of folk songs, together with the descriptions of numerous first encounters (see Chapter 2). It is not even that Léry's account transformed a first encounter into an ethnographic moment that is important for us, but rather that he sensed that the music of Tupinamba ritual was not so very different from the music of his own tradition, which he regarded as beginning with the Greeks and unfolding as a truly Western music history. Léry described a process of growing closer to the music of the Tupinamba, undergoing an aesthetic conversion of his own, from an initial stage in which Tupinamba songs were meaningless to one in which he felt a closeness, even a recognizable kinship:

> At the beginning of this witches' sabbath, when I was in the women's house, I had been somewhat afraid; now I received in recompense such joy, hearing the measured harmonies of such a multitude, and especially in the cadence and refrain of the song.... Whenever I remember it, my heart trembles, and it seems their voices are still in my ears.

(Léry, 1990: 142 and 143)

The accounts generated by and about first encounters are so many and so complex that it would surely have been possible to write this book from them. The justification for doing this lies not only in the wealth of information they contain, but also in the nature of the experiences they narrate. We witness those experiences already in Léry's first encounter: he is present in the first person, but he describes the transformation of that person. There can be no denying that the first encounter was physical and that Léry returned to the encounter through memory made meaningful to him through his body.

It is in the nature of first encounters with world music that our memory of them produces an almost physical return to the encounter itself. This is the nature of musical ethnography, the common practices of physically being present when others are making music, that provides a common thread to the methods shared by ethnomusicology, popular-music and folk-music study, and the other disciplines concerned with world music. Each time we engage in fieldwork, each time we attempt to make sense of musical phenomena that differ from what we know, we return to our own first encounters, sometimes to retrieve information, but most often to remember again what it meant to experience world music for the first time. In this sense, we continue to have first encounters, not least as our sense of the whole of world music is increasingly tempered by experiences with myriad parts. In my own case, both as I embark on new research projects in places I have never before been and as I rethink older projects, I begin by revisiting my first encounters, and by allowing new experiences to accrue to them. My first encounter with the Irish-American farmer Charles Bannen, who sang well over a hundred songs and ballads from oral tradition at his parlour organ, has shaped the ways I have encountered concentration-camp survivors in Israel or elderly Romanians who refuse to forget their modest repertory of Yiddish songs. More recently, my first encounters have been with street musicians and pilgrims, all of whom have collectively reshaped the landscapes of a New Europe with music.

It is important for me to provide the reader with a sense of what first encounters have meant for me, not least because there will be moments in this book, which is not primarily about my own research, in which I draw upon my ethnographic experiences. There will be many more moments in which the encounters I describe are

4

more general, for they are meant to open the spaces of world music so readers may have more intimate and varied encounters of their own. Such encounters actually make the best case for what happens when we experience world music, for, as in the case of Jean de Léry in the mid-16th century, transfiguration, sometimes quite remarkable, accompanies the encounter with music outside our own worlds, transforming it to world music.

First meanings of world music

One of the first things we learn upon encountering world music is that 'music' has different meanings elsewhere in the world. On the one hand, music participates in cultural activities and connects to the world in ways unfamiliar to us. On the other hand, what is understood as 'music' itself might be entirely different, or what we think music to be might not be regarded as such. Knowing what music is and what it does, indeed, may have little to do with categories that seem entirely natural to us. As we encounter world music, therefore, it is important to recognize the need to reckon with different epistemologies and ontologies if we are also to understand what world music can mean in its virtually infinite varieties.

By the epistemology of music we mean its ability to be a part of culture as a whole and thus to acquire meaning in relation to other activities. Examining music cross-culturally, we recognize that religious meaning accrues to music in many ways. Music may serve as a vehicle for shaping the voice of a deity; it may demarcate time so that it is more meaningful for the performance of ritual; music may provide one of many ornaments that make religious practice more attractive; certain domains of music-making (e.g. instrumental music in many religions) may raise images of magic or immorality, thus causing some religions to prohibit music in worship. All these relations with religion, varied as they are, reveal something about music's epistemologies. Were we to examine other types of cultural activity – life-cycle customs, food and material culture, sexuality, etc. – music would possess other epistemological qualities. Music's epistemologies often reveal themselves in musical practice, and it is to understand such epistemological questions in world music more completely that ethnomusicology has adopted approaches from the social sciences, especially from anthropology, with its fundamental concern for cultural context.

The ontologies of world music – music's properties of being a part of a lived-in world – are more likely to reveal themselves in the texts of musical practice. The basic ontological question is simply, What is music? If the question is simple, the answers are not. In fact, world musics have very distinctive and contradictory ontologies. Western ontologies of music, for example, privilege the organization of pitches according to specific systems, in other words, the scales and modes we learn while practising a musical instrument. When we insist that recitation of the Qur'an, however, is music because it makes extensive use of the modes (*maqāmāt*) of Arabic classical music, we impose a Western ontology where it does not belong.

From a Western standpoint, it often seems as if the ontologies of world music are untranslatable, especially because the most fundamental ontological categories in the West treat music as if it were an object, a 'thing' that possesses meaning in and of itself. The language with which we talk about music and the ways in which we interpret it conspire to harden the objectified ontologies of our own music. Music is parsed as pieces or works, with movements and sections, and ultimately with sundry units that become smaller and smaller, making music a collection of larger things composed of smaller things. An ontology derived from understanding music as an object is foreign to many music cultures in the world, where, for example, there may be no equivalent linguistic category for affording identity to pieces and works.

The most extreme instances of world music's ontological complexity are music cultures lacking a word equivalent to the Western concept of music. The musical culture of the largely Muslim Hausa people of northern Nigeria is the classic case of an ontology that contains a considerable vocabulary for distinguishing musicians, musical practices, and instruments, but no word for music itself. Clearly, the panoply of epistemologies and ontologies of world music reveals itself in the ways we talk about music and the words we employ to give meaning to music. The box below contains a list of a few of the countless terms used to ascribe ontological meaning to world music. The point here is not to suggest that such terms are equivalent to the Western 'music', but rather to urge readers to question why seeking equivalent identities usually impedes the discovery of deeper meanings.

Ontologies of world music

balungan: fundamental pitches of the melody in Javanese music, whose identity depends on performance and changing improvisation on different instruments in a gamelan and by the singers performing with it.

candomblé: Afro-Brazilian religion, in which extensive use of ritualized music fuses religious beliefs from the African diaspora, for example from Yoruba religion. So extensive is the presence of music that the term candomblé is used almost synonymously for musical and religious practice.

kriti: melodic skeleton in South Indian (Karnatak) classical music. *Kriti*s might be said to have two ontologies, one idealized as a composed piece representable with written notation, the other realizable through improvisational practices central to Karnatak music.

ma: aesthetic emptiness and silence in Japanese music, perceived as an ontological entity in and of itself, rather than as a space (e.g. 'rest') between sounded music.

musica mundana: music of the spheres, a neo-Platonic concept employed by philosophers to account for music in the harmonic order of the universe.

mūsīqā/mūsīqī: terms borrowed from Greek to refer to musical practices imported into Islamic societies.

qirā'ah: recitation of the Qur'an, literally 'reading' or 'calling'. In Islam never considered to be music.

rasa: an emotional or spiritual condition in Indian music – figuratively the 'taste which one relishes' – attained by proper performance of various attributes, some musical and others extramusical, such as the moods associated with Hindu myth or the time of day.

samā': Arabic word translatable as both 'hearing' and 'listening'. Musical experience in Islam, determined by the perception and reception of sound, rather than by its production.

saṅgīta: Sanskrit word roughly translatable as 'music', but in early theoretical treatises meant to embrace a range of practices that included Brahmanic ceremony, song, instrumental music, dance, and certain types of theatre.

ta'ameh ha-mikrah: recitation of the Hebrew Bible, especially the Torah. In Judaism never considered to be music.

wai khruu: Thai Buddhist performance of ritualized music and dance, which crosses and mediates religious and aesthetic categories.

zikr: Arabic word translatable as both 'memory' and 'remembering'. Sufi ritual in which the Muslim believer draws physically and spiritually closer to God by chanting the name of Allah with ever-increasing intensity.

The diversity of musics in the world has engendered its fair share of epistemological and ontological meanings, ranging from notions that music is fundamentally religious to the common pronouncement that music is a universal language. Such questions interest us throughout the course of this book, not because we shall ever prove them correct or incorrect, but rather because they reflect a desire to endow music with global meaning. Ethnomusicologists generally assert that there is no society in the world without music, thereby attributing universality at a basic epistemological level. Rather than attempt to find empirical evidence for some concept of music that might make it a universal language, a more skeptical modern tradition of scholarship celebrates the differences exhibited by the plethora of musical languages that together constitute world music. The less skeptical postmodern fascination with world music, in contrast, has more commonly relished the possibility that something universal provides the ontological glue that makes world music a reality.

The desire to understand world music as revealing a pathway toward the universal is very powerful, so much so that it can have the inverse effect of levelling difference, in other words, creating the illusion that what we experience as world music is more similar than different. We must also ask ourselves, however, whether the analysis and translation that follow ethnographic encounters do not also reflect a search for similarity, if only to explain the differences to which we struggle to give meaning. At the beginning of the 21st century the search for common epistemologies and ontologies has both positive and negative implications for the ways we perceive the meaning of world music. Or do I mean for the meanings of world musics? The difference is not simply a matter of wordplay, for world music acquires meaning through both individual and collective, local and global, qualities, and sorting these out is anything but easy. It is, nonetheless, the task of this book to show why sorting them out is of singular importance.

First musicians

Musicians, often in quite significant numbers, populate many mythological and religio-philosophical writings about the origins of religion and history – and music. When we reflect, as we did in the previous section, on the complex presence of music in epistemologies and ontologies of other human activities, it is hardly surprising that musicians should be there, indeed as what we here call 'first musicians'. These first musicians occupy the transitional spaces between what is not human and what is, and as musicians they appear in two guises, first as performers and second as craftspeople who fashion the musical instruments they play from the substance of the earth or from the bodies of once-living beings. We witness these first musicians precisely at those mythological moments when identity is most critically called into question, particularly the identities that distinguish sacred realms from secular, and the natural from the artificial. First musicians are usually endowed with the power to call attention to the critical issues of identity and then to offer music as a means of achieving potential solutions. In this way first musicians inscribe music upon the foundation myths of religions throughout history and the world.

Human intervention at the origins of music is no simple matter. In Jewish tradition there are two origin myths, both in the first book of the Torah, *Genesis*. In the fourth chapter, music comes into being associated with two different types of instruments, those made from the bodies of animals and shaped to resemble humans, and those moulded from the elements of the earth. One inventor of music, Yuval, is associated with the first, and another inventor of music, Tubal Cain, is associated with the second. Elsewhere in *Genesis* we encounter the ontology of music at the symbolic centre of one of the most far-reaching of all biblical stories, the *Akedah* or 'Binding of Isaac'. In this story (*Genesis* 22) Abraham shows himself willing to carry out God's commandment to sacrifice his own son, Isaac. Just as Abraham is about to kill his son – he has already raised a knife over Isaac on the sacrificial altar – the voice of God intervenes, informing Abraham that he may substitute a ram trapped in the nearby bushes by his horns. After Abraham has sacrificed and burned the ram, he finds that the animal's horns are left, and he rescues these to use them as the *shofar* that he will bequeath to the Jewish people as the central instrument of ritual. The sounding of the *shofar* gives meaning to time and history, and it sonically represents Jewish identity, which remains traceable even today to the first musicians in *Genesis*.

Gods and goddesses, men and women assume many and varied forms throughout the great epic cycles of Hinduism, and we might assume – correctly – that the first musicians also play a significant number of roles. The first musician appearing with the greatest frequency, not only in the Hindu epic *Mahabhārāta* but also in the visual iconography of music until the present, is Krishna. Krishna represents a constellation of divine qualities, among them divine love and beauty (*prema* and *rupa*), but even more important for his role as a first musician are the many episodes in his life, from his childhood onward, during which he is associated with *gopīs*, the female cowherds, which further symbolize the relation of the soul to god. That relation appears in countless images of Krishna playing the flute to cowherds, in the narratives that accompany Indian modes, or *rāgas*, and iconography used to depict divine love. Krishna's presence as a first musician is general, we might say universalized; in contrast, the goddess Sarasvatī enjoys a more localized presence. In Hindu writings she represents an ontology of human understanding, *vidyā*, that allows the human to transcend the cycle of reincarnation, and it is this ontology that she brings to the most primal of all Indian music instruments, the *vīṇā*. So basic is the meaning of the *vīṇā* to Hinduism that its very physical shape, with a head and vocal cords that sing and a gourd body that resonates as the human body, is regarded as metaphysically human. To enhance Sarasvatī's ability to effect *vidyā*, which we might interpret as the physicality of life's cycles before and after death, she appears frequently in the iconography that appears on *vīṇā*s themselves; the *vīṇā* of Karnatak classical music, in fact, is often referred to as the *sarasvatī vīṇā*. Though a first musician of the first order, Sarasvatī retains her presence in Indian music today, serving as a reminder of music's first meanings.

11

Who's on first: religion, tradition, or aesthetics?

Read in the name of thy Lord who created,
Who created man of blood coagulated.
Read! Thy Lord is most beneficent,
Who taught by the pen,
Taught that which they knew not unto men.
(Qur'an, Surah 96: 1–5)

A revealed work itself, as written text, oral performance, and aural experience, the Qur'an is a revelation of the word of God. Meaning is immanent at many different layers in the Qur'an – the words and the written script in which they appear, the poetic form and the rhythm of the language, the modal and melodic patterns with which they are read and heard, aloud and internally. Meaning is intricate and profound, open to interpretation and yet fully identifiable when perceived in its ultimate singularity. Revelation, perception, and performance are all conflated as experience in Surah 96, in which Mohammad hears the commandment of God through the revelation that Gabriel, as the messenger of God, reveals to the Prophet. It is a case of many meanings coalescing as one, and from the encounter that makes the revelation possible new meaning, which embodies pre-existing meanings, emerges.

I have chosen one of the essential texts of the Qur'an to open this section on aesthetics and world music for several reasons. There is the obvious reason, that the Qur'an is a 'musical' work, which is to say that performance and perception depend on musical context, specifically the modal and melodic traditions of *qirā'ah*, or recitation (also glossed as 'reading' or 'calling', both relevant descriptions of the act of performance). Sacred texts are not infrequently ontological embodiments of performance contexts. It is in the act of reading itself, usually so that both reader and listener can hear the voice revealed through the text, that meaning comes into being. The understanding of meaning, however, is possible only through perception, namely through 'hearing' or 'listening' (*samā'*) to the revealed voice of God in the Qur'an's text. The aesthetic functions of the Qur'an, which are contingent on religious meaning, are ontologically not unique to it, and these lend themselves to comparison with other sacred texts (see Chapter 3).

The recitation of the Qur'an also reveals something very basic about the aesthetics of world music, which will run through this book like a leitmotif. In our encounters with world music, aesthetic issues cannot be isolated and bracketed off. Searching for meaning in the music alone, as if it possessed aesthetic autonomy, will yield only incomplete answers at best, and it will violate the music at worst. The complex aesthetic embeddedness of world music is one of the ways in which it differs radically from Western music. Aesthetic embeddedness is strikingly evident in sacred music, where music's meanings are so often dependent on its ability to do something, to effect change or to bring about transcendence. It is not just that sacred meaning accrues to music because it is transformed to song texts or ritual narratives: sacred music transforms text, narrative, and ritual into meaning. Music possesses the aesthetic power to transform. In her studies of Theravada Buddhism in Thailand Deborah Wong has identified such aesthetic embeddedness in the ceremonial complex called *wai khruu*. Wong observes that

> perhaps most importantly, the transformational aspect of performance is enacted over and over again in the *wai khruu*: teachers are revealed as spirits and deities, children are transformed into dancers and musicians, and each master teacher shows his other face as the sage from the beginning of time.
>
> (Wong, 2001: xxiii)

In Mahayana Buddhism of East Asia music transforms ritual into the political organization of monastic life, in which priests and lay people perform the meanings they encounter in a realm where both the sacred and profane worlds overlap. As Pi-yen Chen has demonstrated through detailed transcriptions of the musical soundscapes of monastic ritual, music realizes the ways in which individuals cohabit these several worlds, allowing the worshipper to perform these worlds simultaneously. We might imagine that all this is a lot to ask of music, but in fact the aesthetic embeddedness of music allows us, even enjoins us, to ask music to transform meaning through performance. The power of music in Buddhism, or for that matter in most religions, resides in the ways its meanings can effect transformation.

We may not often think of power as an aesthetic property, but in this book on world music it appears again and again in that role. At moments of encounter, music possesses power, and it affords power to those who search for meaning. Music's ability to do something is dependent upon the power accruing to it at the various levels of aesthetic embeddedness. It is for this reason, moreover, that encounters with world music so frequently lead to struggles over the appropriation of power. Music is inevitably present at the encounter between the West and its others precisely because power is at stake. In the age of colonialism, for example, sacred music frequently provided a primary text in the encounter between missionaries and those they sought to convert. From the late 16th until the late 18th century Jesuit missionaries were acutely aware of the ways in which music afforded power, and for this reason they created repertories specifically with the intent of opening a space in which conversion, in other words the transformation of spiritual meaning through music, could take place. The spaces of conversion underwent various processes of ritualization, and whereas one might have expected music to be stripped of essential meanings, it was more often opened to the acquisition of new meanings, which grew in power because of their aesthetic differences.

Ritual among the indigenous peoples of the Andes continues to bear witness to the ways in which musical meaning proliferated, producing multiple narratives, each one inscribing a long history of encounter. Musical performance at modern fiestas in the Andes not only contains layer upon layer of meaning, but it provides a ritualized space in which the historical encounters that produced such meaning are performed again. Similarly, Protestant hymnody used in various missionary contexts has undergone transformations in which new meanings yielded the power to indigenize and resist. Hymnody among many Native North American peoples has provided new possibilities for retaining indigenous musical styles and performance contexts, so much so that appropriation must be seen not as stemming from Euro-American cultural domination but as a form of Native American resistance. The transformation of mission hymns to national anthems in Africa is yet another example of the ways in which the aesthetic embeddedness of music transforms meaning. Enoch Mankayi Sontonga's 'Nkosi sikelel'i Afrika' ('God Bless Africa') first came into existence as a hymn, but underwent many transformations on its way to become a pan-African anthem of resistance to colonial domination and then a national anthem for Tanzania in 1964 and South Africa in 1995. In the course of its history, 'Nkosi sikelel'i Afrika' picked up texts in numerous indigenous languages, as well as in English and Afrikaans, which together enhanced its post-colonial significance.

The complex aesthetic questions raised by world music reflect the several ways in which we interpret world music's relation to globalization. Interpreted from one perspective, world music that forms through global encounters loses some measure of what we might perceive as original meaning. Encounter, however, is also a point of origin, for new meaning accrues to world music because of the aesthetic transformations that it sets in play. As we expand our perspectives on world music, we may begin to realize that the encounters that produce it do not primarily create situations in which one side wins and the other loses. The aesthetic complex of world music requires a different set of perspectives. If I might be allowed to play with the metaphors of American baseball, it may not be a question of 'who's on first', rather how to proceed now that the bases are aesthetically loaded.

Charles Seeger, metaphysicist of world music

Why choose Charles Seeger as our first ethnomusicologist? After all, he was not only an ethnomusicologist, and his strong ethnomusicological leanings notwithstanding he preferred to use the more inclusive 'musicology' to ethnomusicology, thereby signalling his unwillingness to eliminate any kind of music from an inclusive and 'unitary' field of musical study. It is not, in fact, always easy to find common threads in the thinking and work of Charles Seeger, but it is the most common thread of all that has led to my choice. In virtually all his writings on music, his activities as a teacher, and his undertakings as a public intellectual, Charles Seeger concerned himself with the identity of world music.

Methodologically, philosophically, and musically, Charles Seeger (1886–1979) could not have been more eclectic. His musical education prepared him to be a composer, while his early predilection as a pedagogue led him to establish music within a broad liberal-arts curriculum. His first encounters with world music came rather later in his life, apparently after he discovered folk music as the 'music of the people'. His fieldwork was no less eclectic than his other undertakings, and though he engaged himself intensively with folk music collecting in the 1930s and 1940s, and then with Latin American music ethnography in the 1940s and 1950s, he largely turned from fieldwork to systematic approaches in the 1950s and 1960s, running experiments on his 'invention', the melograph, a mechanical device for the transcription of musical sound recordings. Though his writings have the reputation for being enigmatic, and despite the fact that he himself never fashioned a book from his diverse writings, Seeger influenced ethnomusicology in the 20th century like no other scholar.

There is, in fact, a discernible core to Seeger's thinking, and the eclectic paths of his diverse activities lead, rather consistently, to that core. In his writing we find an almost obsessive concern with one of the most basic ontological questions about music, its relation to words. Ultimately, this is a concern about musical meaning, in other words, the dilemma that arises when we must use words to talk about music even though words fail to convey musical meaning. Ethnomusicology must confront this dilemma, with, however, little or no hope of overcoming it. Seeger's answer was not to give up, but rather constantly to search for other means to understand the meaning of music. Social contexts were no less important than musical texts; ascribing value to different musics did not exclude the possibilities of measuring their physical and structural properties; recognizing the inadequacies of representational systems was no reason to forge abstract models to represent cognitive processes approximated by music. Seeger did not impose historical and geographical boundaries on music, and by not doing so, he laid the groundwork for studying world music. His influence on the study of music today confirms his vision that, with a growing awareness of the diversity of world music, it would be possible for many to recognize the potential of becoming first ethnomusicologists.

Returning to first: popular encounters with world music

World music has already produced its fair share of popular music stars, and more than a few have achieved mythical proportions. Stardom, in fact, may well form at the crossroads (a term now standard in the vocabulary of worldbeat) formed by a number of myths and mythologies, which together intensify the popularity of world music at the beginning of the 21st century. Perhaps no other worldbeat star has better represented the crossroads of traditional and postmodern myths of world music than Nusrat Fateh Ali Khan (1948–97), the Pakistani singer of *qawwali*, a Hindusthani (i.e. North Indian and Pakistani) devotional music traditionally sung at the shrines of Sufi Muslim saints. The myths about Nusrat Fateh Ali Khan make a great deal of his connection to tradition. Whereas it was indeed the case that his father was also a musician and that he performed with members of his family throughout his life, there is no way of substantiating claims that his was a family of qawwali singers that stretched for six centuries to the very beginnings of Sufism in Pakistan and northern India. His understanding of the musical structure and formal poetics of qawwali demonstrates itself fully in many early recordings, but it seems to lose meaning in the fusion experiments of many later recordings and in the tracks he recorded for films such as *Dead Man Walking* and *The Last Temptation of Christ*, which nonetheless contributed enormously to his stardom and to the popularity of qawwali.

Transformation characterized every level of Nusrat Fateh Ali Khan's career – from sacred to secular, classical to popular, traditional to fusion, devotional to public – and it would therefore seem that his was a life in which the distance between qawwali as a Muslim devotional music and qawwali as popular world music grew ever greater, to the point that the global erased the local. Such an interpretation, however, would miss the crucial point. Nusrat Fateh Ali Khan did not abandon the devotional qualities of qawwali, and he was aware that concert performances communicated different meanings than did performances at shrines. He expressed his awareness of such distinctions between the traditional and the popular very clearly in interviews. He was also known to give alternative concerts in more devotional settings when on tour. He was profoundly conscious of the difference between the ways in which music functioned within Sufism and 'Sufi music'. It is that difference that will afford a leitmotif for interpreting the popular repertories and practices of world music that runs through this book.

As a complex of sectarian and communitarian practices within Islam, Sufism historically developed as a component of a world religion. Sufi sects formed wherever Islam spread, and for the most part these acculturated local musics were used in Muslim worship. Sufism embellished religious practice within Islam. In a religion that depends essentially on the centralization of certain beliefs and sacred texts, Sufism formed at the peripheries, where it accommodated alterity and change. At the end of the 20th century, in part as a component of Islam's political presence in post-colonial Muslim nations and in part because of the globalization of religion, Sufism has, in and of itself, become a world religion. Sufism, in other words, is no longer solely a set of sectarian practices within Islam, but an expressive system throughout the world, the tenets and practices of which can be embraced by Muslims and non-Muslims alike. Emblematic of this transformation is the growing frequency of the term 'Sufi music' as a self-standing, aesthetic category of world music, which is advertised, marketed, and consumed as popular music (see, for example, Figure 1). Sufi music has come to express the aesthetic core of globalized Sufism, but in so doing it has become dislodged from many traditional Sufi practices. Through Sufi music's separation from Sufism and the aesthetic critique of religious practice, it has acquired a powerful

WE ARE THE SOUND!

1. **CDs of Sufi music on display in a record shop in Salzburg, Austria (1996)**

new set of meanings. It has been freed from the strictures of musical style and religious function. The ontological and epistemological meanings of Sufi music as popular music at the beginning of the 21st century are fundamentally aesthetic.

Again, we witness the contradictions evident in the two different responses to globalization and world music. There is one set of perspectives that welcomes the rise and spread of popular Sufi music as an historical process accompanying much that is positive, say, religious revival in general and Islamic fundamentalism in particular. Another set of perspectives perceives negative implications in the same historical process. Is Sufi music a new music and an innovative set of practices with a traditional basis, or does it negate traditional sounds and functions by buying into the world-music market? Both responses have led to a great deal of theorizing in the last decade and a half. The problem with much theorizing about worldbeat, however, is that it has treated the changes following upon the heels of the appropriation and dissemination of world music as popular music moving only in one direction. Again, Nusrat Fateh Ali Khan provides a case-in-point for multiple rather than single directions, for it is indeed the case that he continued to play qawwali with deeply Muslim meanings, even distinguishing this from other music he played in concert. American Muslims whom I interviewed in the 1990s found deeply spiritual meaning in worldbeat qawwali, while at the same time they were intensely aware of how qawwali was appropriated and marketed. For these Muslims, the attraction of a qawwali as popular music did not eliminate the spiritual power of Islam. Quite the contrary, popular qawwali led them back to that power.

At the beginning of the 21st century it has become possible to speak of both the history and historicity of world music. The historical trajectory of world music is largely characterized by return and revival. 'Sufi Music' in the world music context does not hesitate to participate in the revivalism within Islam or to return to the veneration of a genealogy of saints, many of whom, like the

13th-century poet, musician, and Sufi, Amir Khusrau, played an active role in the establishment of musical traditions. The seven-century historical-genealogical distance between Amir Khusrau and Nusrat Fateh Ali Khan is closed by Sufi music. Return and revival appear wherever we look at popular world musics emerging from traditional contexts. In a different part of the Islamic world, for example, the popular Turkish music *arabesk* offers its critique of modern Turkish society by nostalgically returning to earlier popular styles, but also to regional folk musics from the countryside and to sacred traditions with Islamic contexts. It is the sound of all these musics forged as a new aesthetic that accounts for arabesk's enormous popularity today.

The historical tradition of world music thus radically contrasts with the teleological history of Western art music – indeed, of the Euro-American mainstream in general – a history that unfolds through stylistic development and a genealogy of 'Great Men', each of whom passes the torch of tradition to a successor. In world music, tradition returns again and again, not to be used up or relegated to the past, but to be restored with new meanings in the present. The resulting historicity bears comparison with several 20th-century critiques of modernity, notably Martin Heidegger's concept of *Wiederholung* (repetition) in history and Jacques Derrida's philosophical dismantling of tradition (*déconstruction*). As it becomes popular music, world music appropriates the past and tradition to effect a radical break with them. The great paradox – a paradox that we shall follow through this book – is that popular music re-establishes the conditions of encounter because its historicity, marked by return and fuelled by revival, also reinstates encounter. Local musicians become dependent on the global music industry. Traditional melody and functions must undergo transformation in order to be mapped on Western harmony and repackaged for global consumption.

The question, however, is whether this post-colonial and postmodern encounter is effectively different from any earlier encounter. Does the explosion of popular world music, instead, renew one of the deepest meanings of world music, the recognition by local musicians that subversion of or resistance to hegemony is made possible only by encounter? To answer such questions, we too must proceed historically by returning to past encounters that are most meaningful for world music today.

Chapter 2
The West and the world

World music for the record

In the early history of folk music research and ethnomusicology, scholars doing fieldwork were often photographed organizing their collections and making their recordings. In several notable cases, these photographs have become icons for the collection and study of world music. There they are, the ancestors of today's ethnomusicologists and today's performers of world music, encountering each other and locked in the exchange of cultural knowledge (see Chapter 7). In Figure 2, the distinguished ethnomusicologist Frances Densmore, whose collections embraced as many of North America's indigenous peoples as possible, sits in 1916 with the Blackfoot Indian, Mountain Chief, in Washington, DC, where he will sing to her, and she will reduce his song to traces on the map of Native American music. In Figure 3, a postcard published on the eve of World War II, the French folk song collector and priest Louis Pinck (1873–1940) records the 'almost one-hundred year-old Mama Türk', singing 'ancient songs' for the wax-cylinder recorder on 29 April 1938 in the village of Steinbiedersdorf, Alsace-Lorraine.

Innumerable questions have been posed about such photographs, the representations of a moment of ethnographic encounter in the history of world music. Are they meant to illustrate a sort of equality

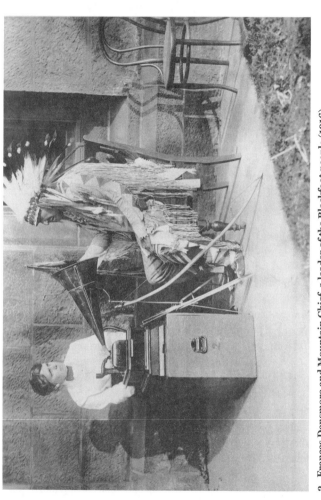

2. Frances Densmore and Mountain Chief, a leader of the Blackfoot people (1916)

shared by fieldworker and consultant? Does the recording device separating them assure us of authenticity? What does the presence of mediating technology tell us about the 'field' in which this ethnographic encounter takes place? Are we witnessing a transfer of ownership, from musician to recording and transcription? Finally, is not the real issue here the unequal distribution of power, in other words, the use of technological means of representation to strip the 'native' of music and appropriate it for the enjoyment, study, and consumption of those who do not own the music but do own the technology to possess it?

3. **Louis Pinck and Mama Türk**

Two questions about power – its use and abuse – lie at the heart of the present chapter. The first question has particularly expansive dimensions, for it asks about the ways in which concepts of world music, in the past and the present, not only reflect but encourage the division of the world between those with and those without power. It strikes at the core of one of the dilemmas in the history of world music: why does world music so often drive a wedge between the West and the rest? The second question seemingly asks us to search for answers at the more local level, for it concerns the tools and products that make the imagination and study of world music possible. It forces us to confront the dilemma of ownership: just what does happen when a transcription or recording of someone else's music appears in print or on record as world music? Who gains power from the act of representation? Who loses it? Such questions are anything but new. Indeed, they may be inextricably bound to the history and, more disturbingly, methodology of world music.

I now turn to a set of related case studies that provide answers to the two questions about power that this chapter poses. Though the primary actor in both case studies, Erich Moritz von Hornbostel (1877–1935), one of the nestors of German comparative musicology, is the same, the recorded anthologies expose fundamentally different models of world music, models that were evident in the first printed anthologies of world music (e.g. Herder's two volumes of folk songs) and in the most recent anthologies of world music, released on CDs or through the Internet, consumed for their educational and entertainment value. Before we reach the Grammy Awards for world music, it behoves us to look at the first attempts to put world music on record.

The two anthologies examined here together constituted the first attempts by an ethnomusicologist to respond to what I call the 'anthological impulse': gathering together diversity on record in order to represent world music in a holistic way. Although Erich Moritz von Hornbostel organized and edited – anthologized, one really should say – both projects, they differ in some very distinctive ways. In the most basic sense the two anthologies have different audiences, which is also to say different users and consumers. In the opening sections of this chapter I wish to suggest that basic differences have continued to characterize world music anthologies up to the present, and in so doing they have come to signify one of the essential dilemmas, even contradictions, that we face when we study and teach world music.

If we think of Hornbostel's *Demonstration Collection* (1963) and *Music of the Orient* (1979, orig. 1934) as the 'first anthologies on record', it is to make some larger points about the anthological impulse as a persistent theme in the history of world music. That theme draws our attention to a number of issues having to do with mediation: between collector and collected; between those unable to represent themselves and those with the economic and technological capital to do so; between scholars and lay people; between private practice and public display; between humanistic fascination and exotic fantasy. Hornbostel's anthologies together made an important first step toward using the anthology for more than simply archiving field recordings, making them available (1) to scholars for study and (2) to a broader audience for popular consumption.

The scientific and the popular often split into two sides separated by a mediational divide. On one side we witness the primary concerns of the early comparative musicologists. The anthologies contain examples that clearly served as gateways to understanding music's origins and authenticity. The listener navigates the anthology using a comparative map; at every new outpost something new accrues to the world music traveller's knowledge of music's immanent diversity. Other early concerns of the comparative musicologists also come into play, for example the diffusion of music as an object of culture and the formation of 'cultural regions' (*Kulturkreise* in German, the basis for a school of anthropological thinking in the early 20th century). It was the goal of the anthologizers to use music to chart maps of the world in new ways.

On the other side of the mediational divide we witness the representational language of *fin-de-siècle* fantasies of the exotic. Stated simply, the anthologies are also repositories of strangeness, whose attraction is their absence of familiarity. The maps of world music constructed by the two Hornbostel anthologies look, on their surfaces, quite different. The *Demonstration Collection* views world music from the bottom up; *Music of the Orient* views world music from the top down. In the first anthology we encounter a welter (42) of very brief examples, often performed by anonymous performers at the farthest reaches of ethnological study. Even the examples from Europe come from repertories that were regarded as very old and prehistorical (for example track 1 is Swiss yodelling, and track 3 comes from the Caucasus). Distinguishing the 'Orient' on the second anthology are practices of art music, which require the greater sophistication of larger ensembles and longer works. There are fewer examples (24) on the second set, even though it also contains two LPs, and many of these are extracts or movements from larger works.

Both anthologies bear witness to historical concepts, but again we find that history in the *Demonstration Collection* begins primarily with the oldest – and by extension most authentic and exotic – examples and unfolds along a path toward greater complexity, whereas in the second anthology Hornbostel follows the Orientalist model of history, which G. W. F. Hegel and 19th-century European historians had systematized, in which 'civilization' moves from east to west (i.e. from the East to the West). World music history in the first anthology is, therefore, inclusive, embracing the most isolated music culture in Oceania and the *longue durée* of European traditions. But music narrates an exclusive world history for the Orient, moving along a single path along which progress is intrinsic to separating people with history from those without history.

The *Demonstration Collection*

The *Demonstration Collection* is inclusive in another way, which is not irrelevant to the distinctions of world music that we examine in this book: it includes the work of scholars, as well as of colonial officials and missionaries, who were committed to documenting the earliest forms of music and then transforming these into a

4. (**Phonogr.-Nr.** 19 = 48) *nkan*, Gesang beim Seelenfest. Vorsänger: Ngi-Nkompfa; Chor (Jünglinge) unison, in 48. in Oktaven (außer in Takt 2).

Cylinder 86 — Demonstrations-Sammlung Nr. 86

4. Funeral chant of the Pangwe people (1913)

comprehensive scientific discourse. Despite the fact that the history of the *Demonstration Collection* stretches across almost an entire century and serves also as a prosopography (collective history) of the most important early school of ethnomusicological research (Berlin) and the most distinguished scholars of the 20th century, it has proved difficult to uncover the details of the anthology itself. The recorded examples themselves come entirely from the period 1900–13. The *Demonstration Collection* employed representational and rhetorical languages that were systematic and comparative, in a word, scientific. Note this in Figure 4, which contains a transcription with quite exacting ethnographic and musical detail of cylinder 86 from the German version of the *Demonstration Collection* (LP 2, side B, cut 4 of the 1963 Folkways reissue).

Music of the Orient

There was no equivocating when it came to stating that the goals of *Music of the Orient* were different from those of the *Demonstration Collection*. By the early 1930s, monographs and more popular studies of world music had begun to appear in significant numbers, spurred on by the popularization of humanistic scholarship in general. Recordings, too, had won a new place in the public sphere during the 1920s, creating new audiences who possessed gramophones in their homes. *Music of the Orient*, released on the Odeon and Parlophone labels (at the time German and English transnational recording labels), intentionally meant to take advantage of these several transformations in the consumption of music.

If it were just a matter that *Music of the Orient* competed economically for the place never quite occupied by the *Demonstration Collection* – sales of the earlier anthology dropped off entirely once *Music of the Orient* appeared – the story of these two anthologies would be much simpler. *Music of the Orient* told a different story and narrated a different history of world music, and it did so by anthologizing in a different way, exemplified in Figure 5, an 'art-song' from Tunis, in *'maqām mezmūm'*.

In more ways than one, the two recorded anthologies represent African musics that were geographically, ontologically, and historically entirely unlike each other. Whereas the *Demonstration Collection* places considerable emphasis on sub-Saharan Africa, an object of colonial desire for Germany in the pre-World War I era, *Music of the Orient* considers only North Africa. The site of collecting for the former is the 'field' and 'mission station', where very specific types of cultural work were being done, with which comparative musicology was collaborating. The site of collecting in North Africa is 'the town', the cosmopolitan centre where both Andalusian (i.e. quasi-medieval European) and modern European (i.e. the violin, which Hornbostel assures the reader is 'European')

Tunis

23. Art-song. *Maqām Mezmūm*

The ancient view of life places the life of man as well as all earthly events—microcosmos—in counter-relation to a path of deified stars, seasons and hours of the day—macrocosmos. The music, too, is included in the harmony of the cosmos; the harmony adopts the personality of the planetary deity represented in the leading tone; this type of composition demands a proper time and occasion of delivery in order to bring about bliss and not destruction. Maqām Mezmūm calls the demons—but woe if the call resounds inside the house!

The ancient faith and customs have, in the "Andalusian" style—originating in the Moorish Period of Granada—been more purely preserved in the north-western towns of Africa than in the East. This Tunisian recording belongs to this style. A European violin alternates with the vocalist in the melody, a lute ('Ud) accompanies (see recording 19). The metrically timed song is preceded by a rhythmically free structure, which displays the characteristic feature of the Maqām: the leading tone at the base of the structural treble (Do-Modus), the accentuated "Neutral" third (halving the treble) and principally the fundamental theme:

Tonal structure * :

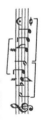

Town Players. Photo: Dr. R. Lachmann.

5. 'Art-song' from Tunis, in *maqām mezmūm*

influences mix with the 'ancient view of life'. Hornbostel was not himself the collector, but his Berlin colleague in ethnomusicology, Robert Lachmann, was. The musical others who inhabit these very different sites could not contrast more with each other. Or could they? In fact, we witness in both cases that the musicians are travelling along an historical track that brings them close to the West, either through conversion to Christianity in sub-Saharan Africa or through the demolition of the borders between Europe and North Africa in the Tunisian art-song, which would play an important role in the 1932 Cairo Congress of Arab Music (see Chapter 3).

The two different Africas also reveal two different discourses and two different types of ethnomusicological work. In the *Demonstration Collection* Hornbostel and the colleagues whose work he weaves into the fabric of his anthology forge the representational tools for comparative musicology, which depend on and then generate scientism and an awareness of world music as the product of cultural difference. The traces of a scientific approach are still quite evident in *Music of the Orient*, but they are used in other ways. The anthology itself becomes a site for spectatorship, through its emphasis on the visual and on music drama, and for world music as entertainment, through its gestures to cosmopolitan consumers. At the beginning of the 21st century these two broad generic categories dominate world music anthologies no less than they did in the early 1930s.

Recording, collecting, and anthologizing the other

Early collections that included representative anthologies of folk music

• Johann Gottfried Herder, '*Stimmen der Völker in Liedern*' and *Volkslieder* (1778 and 1779). Two volumes that gathered folk songs from around the world (see Chapter 5).

• Achim von Arnim and Clemens Brentano, *Des Knaben Wunderhorn* (1806 and 1808). Anthologies of 'folk poetry', lacking melodies, but with texts that would become the canon of Central European folk song in the 19th century.

• John Philip Sousa, *National, Patriotic and Typical Airs of All Lands* (1890). Produced during an historical moment of growing American colonial expansion, the 'Band Master of the US Marine Corps' published a volume of songs in detailed transcriptions and arrangements that maps music on the world (see Chapter 5).

Early attempts to use recording technology to gather world music

• The Chicago World's Columbian Exposition of 1893. The first attempt to use wax cylinders to record the music of different music cultures. The 103 recordings include Javanese, Turkish/Levantine, and Kwakiutl musics, as well as examples from the 'South Sea Islands' exhibit at the Chicago World's Fair.

• A. Z. Idelsohn, *Thesaurus of Hebrew-Oriental Melodies*, vols 1–5 (1913–29). Using recording devices from the Austro-Hungarian Academy of Sciences, collected and transcribed the music of Jews from throughout the diaspora.

• Wilhelm Doegen (ed.), *Unter fremden Völkern – Eine neue Völkerkunde* (1925). Transcriptions and analyses of songs, narratives, and linguistic experiments conducted in World War I prisoner-of-war camps by the Germans.

Recording spearheaded by early ethnomusicologists

• Frances Densmore, recordings and transcriptions in multiple volumes, published largely by the Bureau of American Ethnology and the Library of Congress. During a period of more than half a century (1901 until her death in 1957) Densmore moved systematically from one Native American people to the next, using recordings to encompass the full range of their musical cultures (see Figure 2).

• Erich Moritz von Hornbostel, *Demonstration Collection* (1963) and *Music of the Orient* (1979, orig. 1934). Anthologies with recordings that represent cross-sections of world music.

• Cairo Congress of Arab Music 1932. Recordings of music from throughout the 'Arab world', stretching from Morocco in the west to Iraq in the east. The anthology bears witness to ethnomusicological classification, not least because of the conceptual input of Robert Lachmann (see Chapter 3).

Late 20th-century series devoted to world music

• Folkways Records. During much of the second half of the 20th century Moses Asch made his Folkways label (also Ethnic Folkways) available to musicians and music collectors from around the world. Because he was able to keep his recordings – numbering well over 1,000 – in print and circulation, Asch used recordings to expand the availability of world music. The Folkways label is in part maintained by the Smithsonian Institution, which re-releases some early recordings and continues to issue new CDs.

• New World Records. A set of recordings deliberately encompassing all musics of America. The first set of 100 recordings was available around the time of the American Bicentennial in 1976, with continuous production following until the present.

• UNESCO World Music Collection. A recording project that provided counterpoint to the expansion of the United Nations after World War II. Appearing on different labels to evoke a sense of democratic production, the UNESCO recordings are generally anthologies of music from a single nation or region. Classical and traditional musics are emphasized, and many endangered examples are preserved.

Musicians of the Middle Passage

The world musicians that I discuss at the midpoint in this chapter are by and large anonymous: I have no choice but to refer to them collectively as 'Musicians of the Middle Passage'. The Middle Passage was the geographical designation of the journey from Africa to slavery in North and South America, and in Europe and its colonies. It marked the historical and cultural distance between the West and the others created during the Age of Discovery, which persisted through the Age of Enlightenment and beyond to the modern and post-colonial eras, and still farther beyond into the cultural landscapes of the African diaspora (see Chapter 6). The Middle Passage marked a space in which alterity was not just created but enforced through the exercise of power. It was also a space in which world music was and, in the racial imagination, is forged.

Modern scholars are not without records of the musicians of the Middle Passage, but they were almost entirely written by individuals with names and power, for example ship captains, colonial officials, and, as we saw at the beginning of Chapter 1, missionaries. In contrast, the musicians themselves are nameless and stereotyped, even though they frequently attracted attention through their seeming propensity for music-making. The nameless musicians of the Middle Passage illustrate the ways in which the West has historically dominated by enforcing the anonymity of others. The music of the Middle Passage, too, remained nameless, characterized in the records for its lack of nuance and for its stereotypical movements. Even when favourably described – and it surely behoved those who wished to convert the Africans in the new worlds made by Europe to emphasize positive attributes – the music of slaves was celebrated because the melodies were, as Alexander Barclay remarked in 1826, 'simple' and 'lively': 'All is life and joy, and certainly it is one of the most pleasing sights that can be imagined.'

More often than not, however, those invested with more power to record the position of the West in world history, such as Hegel, also writing in the mid-1820s, found it impossible to comprehend any such position for Africans:

> The African, in his undifferentiated and concentrated unity, has not yet succeeded in making this distinction between himself as an individual and his essential universality, so that he knows nothing of an absolute being which is other and higher than his own self.
>
> (Georg Wilhelm Friedrich Hegel, cited in Eze, 1997: 127)

African music did survive the Middle Passage, and in the course of world music history, that music, indeed in the form of the popular musics of the West during the past century and a half, has shaped and influenced world music perhaps more than any other. Among the few possessions many forced to travel the Middle Passages were allowed to bring with them were musical instruments, and these were used to bridge the gap between Africa and the West. African musics developed into a boundless spectrum of genres and forms, through isolation of distinctive markers of selfness and the creative hybridization of otherness. The names of these musics, performed at earlier historical moments by the musicians of the Middle Passage, are found on almost every page of this book, and they would surely dominate any glossary of world music terms. The greatest legacy of the musicians of the Middle Passage might well be the erasure of anonymity and its replacement with a form of power invested in world music and its modern history.

The West and the fissures between 'self' and 'other'

The space between the West and its others has vexed ethnomusicology since its inception. Indeed, we might even go so far as to say that the field has developed by attempting to shape the types of encounter that occur within this space and thus define the space. Depending on the historical moment and the disciplinary focus, it becomes the space between 'high' and 'low' culture, 'oral' and 'literate' culture, 'popular' and 'élite', peoples 'with history' and those 'without history', 'premodern' and 'modern', or, in our own age, 'modern' and 'postmodern'. The paradox here becomes even more troubling when we realize that all these terms and the conceptual pairs they form have distinctly Western origins. Within the pairs one term is available for the observer, transforming the other into a place occupied by the observed.

The dilemma posed for ethnomusicology by this fissure between self and other is all-too-obvious, all the more so because it is a dilemma fraught with moral and ethical implications. Does ethnomusicology's power to represent depend on the others it encounters? Does the acuity and authenticity of representation depend on heightening the degree of alterity, which by extension depends on expanding, if not exaggerating, the fissure? Does a representational vocabulary grounded in alterity actually contribute to the invention of the 'other'?

For ethnomusicology the implications of this fissure are indeed powerful. Ethnomusicologists cannot simply observe and describe the space between self and other, but rather they must enter it and deal with the complex forms of encounter that take place in it. The space opens as the place in which fieldwork occurs. The acts of representation described in this chapter reshape the place between self and other. The ethnomusicologist, all too often, is not alone in the field, and similarly the motivations of the ethnomusicologist in the field may not be singular. To enter the space between self and other is possible only upon acquiring power. The history of ethnomusicology, nonetheless, is distinctive because there has been considerable recognition of the implications of power for the exercise of praxis.

The history of ethnomusicology has unfolded as a response to the dilemma posed by the fissure between the West and its others, by attempting to close it and even to heal the human devastation that it sometimes causes. The point here is not to deny culpability for the abuses that arise because of the fissure, but rather to suggest that ethnomusicology is perhaps notable because of its recognition that closing the fissure was not simply an intellectual advantage but also a moral imperative. Whether individual scholars or approaches were successful in doing so or not is another story.

Attempts to redefine the space between the West and its others have produced a series of historiographic transformations, in effect paradigm shifts that unleashed new encounters with and interpretations of world music. One of the most sweeping of the early paradigm shifts was the direct result of Johann Gottfried Herder's publication of two volumes of folk songs in 1778 and 1779. In his formulation of 'folk song' Herder argued that all people communicated through music as naturally as through speech. By gathering folk songs from as far afield as possible he therefore created a space in which one common cross-section of the world's music would bring human beings – which for Herder meant enlightened human beings – together.

The space that a generalized concept of folk song could represent was enormously influential on the generations that followed Herder. In attempting to collect and publish folk songs to fill that space, however, his successors in the 19th century hardened its boundaries, not least by equating them with linguistic fields and nationalist aspirations. The *Volk* of folk song ceased referring to 'people' – Germans began to substitute the plural *Völker*, which possessed more universal meaning – and began to specify 'nation'. Whereas Herder did not employ the political-geographical designation 'German' to his 18th-century concept of folk song, it became the rule rather than the exception to apply it in the 19th century. The dilemma of West and rest, so ambitiously attacked by Herder, arose again in the generations that followed him.

The employment of mechanical reproduction as a means of recording world music also initially closed the gap. Almost from the first attempts to record world music on wax cylinders it became apparent that the recording device redefined the space between self and other by its very presence in that space. One could bring the 'field' to the cylinder recorder at world's fairs and international expositions, or one could take the cylinder recorder to the field. Though massive in comparison to present-day DAT and minidisc recorders, cylinder recorders were distinctive precisely because of their portability. They could, theoretically, capture music anywhere in the world, effectively negating the space between the West and its others.

The power of portable recording devices to collapse the difference between self and others is one of the mantras of globalization. Again, however, we witness the insistent presence of the key word, 'power'. At the beginning of the 21st century, that persistence has not been lost upon a new generation of ethnomusicologists who are not themselves from the West and whose perspectives have coalesced in new approaches to fieldwork and the field, which have been consistently critical of the implications of Western biases that have refused to disappear. These 'other ethnomusicologies', as they are increasingly called, are not particularly sanguine about the potential of the field to heal such fissures. The space between the West and its others persists not because of the shifting geographies of global encounter but rather because of an endemic imbalance of power. If the space will not close because it cannot close, it therefore becomes incumbent upon ethnomusicology to critique not only the music that it encompasses but also the very notions of selfness that have shaped the encounters of ethnomusicologists with their others.

Johann Gottfried Herder and the invention of world music

With a single act of naming Johann Gottfried Herder (1744–1803) invented world music. It was Herder who coined the term *Volkslied* (folk song), applying it not only to the music he heard in the local world close at hand, but also to a diverse range of repertories that were encountered throughout the world of Enlightenment Europe.

Herder's extensive writings on music formed around three broad themes: folk song, language, and history. Herder imagined folk songs not only as discrete objects, the songs he published in two seminal volumes – the first volume (1778) was entitled 'Voices of the People in Songs', the second volume (1779) simply 'Folk Songs' – but also as a constitutive process of human communication. In one of his most influential early writings on language, Herder held that the origin of speech and song were one, which meant, then, that all humans made music as part of expressing themselves and the distinctive characteristics of the cultures they shared with others. The commonality of speech and song, moreover, contributed significantly to the history of a people, intersecting to shape the development of literacy, religious practice, and responses to other cultures.

Would it be an exaggeration to describe Herder as an ethnomusicologist? He was, at the very least, a polymath, who was equally at home in theology, philosophy, linguistics, and the enlightened study of history and culture. His interest in music, moreover, cut across the disciplines he mustered as a polymath. The son of a Protestant church musician (*Kantor*) in rural East Prussia, Herder developed an early passion for the songs of the church and particularly local hymn-singing, in which oral and written traditions intersected. Herder was not simply an amateur musician, for during the course of his life he wrote music himself, he collaborated with composers (notably J. C. F. Bach, a son of J. S. Bach) and court musicians by writing texts for them, and he incorporated musical themes into his own lyrical poetry, which then found its way into settings by many composers, among them Beethoven, Schubert, Brahms, and Richard Strauss. There is considerable evidence to support a view that Herder was able to develop an ethnographic sensitivity. The first traces of what would become a sustained interest in folk song, for example, are evident in his 1770 meeting with Goethe in Strasbourg exactly during the period when Goethe was gathering Alsatian folk songs, subsequently to be recorded in what has been regarded by German folklorists as one of the very first anthologies produced through fieldwork. Herder himself took a special interest in folk songs collected at the peripheries of German-speaking Europe, and traditions from Estonia and Latvia – his first position was in a church in Riga – occupy a very visible position in his collections of folk song.

Herder's role as an inventor of world music has also acquired significance because of its influence on several critical areas of Enlightenment thought and then beyond on the Romantic and modernist development of that thought. To Herder are attributed several fundamental critical formulations of nationalism; 19th- and 20th-century scholars extended his arguments about folk music to national music and ethnic music. As an inventor of world music, Herder thus raises issues about the West and the rest, about folk music as reflective of European history or of world history. In fact, Herder's writings about music are remarkable for their expansiveness; German folk music is considerably less important to him than many musics at the peripheries of Europe and beyond. The point, here, is not to defend Herder against detractors and misinterpreters, rather to point to the simple historical fact that Western attitudes toward folk music and world music changed dramatically after Herder. If the map he sketched for his philosophy of history emanated from his vantage point as an intellectual in Central Europe, it nonetheless stretched across the entire world, and it displayed an impressive level of detail, not least of which was afforded by the language of music shared by the folk, the people and the nations of the world, all of whom Herder urged his readers to know better through their music.

World Music Grammy Award winners: two portraits

World music has been repeatedly invented and reinvented since the time of Herder. There have been new acts of naming and nuanced representations of new sounds and repertories. Collecting and recording became more efficient and discursive networks more effective. Two centuries after Herder, as we witness throughout this book, there is a great deal that passes as world music. With rather selective examples, moreover, this chapter has shown the persistent presence of scholars, from early polymaths to latter-day ethnomusicologists, in the field, whose excursions and ethnographic journeys brought them into contact with the others whose music they sought to preserve by and for the record.

Scholars were not the only ones whose journeys into the space between the West and the rest were motivated by the urge to record and disseminate world music. We witnessed this in our encounter with musicians of the Middle Passage, whose lives and music were described by ship's captains, colonial officials, and missionaries. The story is scarcely different in the 20th century, during which the production and consumption of recording became big business. If, in fact, the potential for selling world music recordings was tentatively realized during the first half of the century, the production of world music on record accelerated rapidly at mid-century, fully crossing over to the commercial recording industry during the final quarter-century. The sale of world music, first on commercial LPs and since around 1990 on CDs, has become big business, and as such it has introduced new conditions to the ways in which the collecting and recording create an imbalance of power between the West and its others. As in the Enlightenment, neologisms provide evidence for the latest re-imaginings of world music. If *Volkslied* was capaciously inclusive in Herder's coinage, so too are 'worldbeat', 'global pop', and, yes, 'world music' for the recording industry.

This chapter began with a comparative portrait of the two earliest anthologies of world music, and it will end in similar fashion. It would be quite impossible to claim that the two recordings with which I am closing are, in contrast with Hornbostel's two sets, the 'latest anthologies' of world music, for it has become quite impossible to keep pace with the production of new world music anthologies. The two recordings I examine in this final section, however, lend themselves to comparison for different reasons. Both approach world music historically, so much so that the scope of the world they include would be quite unimaginable without taking a perspective that verges on historicist. Both muster performances by many different musicians, albeit for different reasons; the two projects reveal different facets of the key word 'various artists' that accompanies even (or especially) the most commercial recordings of world music. Finally, there is an even more basic reason for examining these two recordings together: both won Grammy Awards and therefore suggest ways of understanding how the record industry itself has come to locate its products between the West and its others.

Santiago – best world music album 1997

Prior to the Age of Discovery, Santiago de Compostela symbolized the western edge of the world known to Europeans. For all intents and purposes the pilgrimage to Santiago defined the West, and it did so by reminding the European Christian that beyond the West lay the unknown. Because pilgrims from throughout the medieval West converged at Santiago after long journeys marked and measured by song and worship, the pilgrimage centre in what is now Galicia in northwestern Spain was also a site of world music. The musical practices that accompanied the medieval pilgrims found their way to written collections, which, too, embodied a cross-section and consolidation of world music, albeit at the western edge of the medieval world.

By choosing to record an album devoted to the pilgrimage to Santiago de Compostela, the well-known Irish traditional band the Chieftains both followed and detoured from the medieval road to the western edge of the world. Among the first advocates of worldbeat Celticism (see Chapter 4), the Chieftains charted a late 20th-century journey with Celtic music, thus transforming Santiago into the centre of the Celtic world. Galicia, the cultural region in which Santiago is located, has increasingly provided the

Celticist imagination with new territory into which to extend the Celtic fringe of Europe, effectively defining Europe's western littoral from north to south as Celtic. The musical journey of the Chieftain's *Santiago*, however, does not move in only one, centripetalizing direction toward Santiago, rather it spins centrifugally out into the world of Galician and Celtic music, inviting other world music sojourners to join the journey. At Guadalupe in Mexico, today the largest pilgrimage centre in the world, the Chieftains are joined by the band Los Lobos and by Linda Ronstadt (cut 8). Uilleann and Galician *gaita* bagpipers join in a polka (cut 6), which provides secular counterpoint for medieval chant (cut 1) and Asturian sacred song (cut 3). For two pieces from Cuba (cuts 12 and 13), Ry Cooder takes *mandola* in hand, weaving Afro-Cuban sounds from lands not yet imagined by medieval pilgrims in their journey to the west.

Santiago had all the earmarks necessary for a Best World Music Grammy in 1997. It combined traditional with popular styles; its multiple artists symbolized an engagement with the world as a whole. In addition to the unknown folk musicians who played along the road to Santiago, there were big-name crossover stars touted by the National Academy of Recording Arts and Sciences for rescuing world music talent from the oblivion of not appearing on record; it was surely not insignificant to the success of *Santiago* in the Grammy voting that Ry Cooder had already twice won Best World Music Grammys for collaborations with V. M. Bhatt (1993) and Ali Farka Toure (1994); for that matter, the Chieftains had twice won Grammys for Best Traditional Folk Recording in 1992 and 1993. The path of medieval pilgrims wending their way to Santiago de Compostela was hardly a mystery by the time the Chieftains and other world musicians travelled it in the mid-1990s; it was firmly in the grasp of the recording industry of the West, and it inscribed a Celtic vision on record that was just familiar and exotic enough to epitomize the space of world music between the West and its others.

Anthology of American Folk Music – best historical recording 1998

By reformatting, reissuing, and reimagining Harry Smith's *Anthology of American Folk Music* in 1997, the Smithsonian Institution contributed a significant chapter to the history of world music. The 'America' of Smith's original Folkways recordings from the 1950s both was and was not synonymous with the 'world' of world music. Harry Smith's original project had differed from that of many who relied on Moses Asch's vision of the world and turned to his studio in the post-World War II era. A polymath of extraordinary and eccentric proportions, Harry Smith assembled his anthology by gathering old commercial recordings, ranging from ethnic and 'race' labels to obscure local companies and 78s that were little more than vanity productions.

In a remarkable number of ways, Harry Smith was a 20th-century intellectual cousin of Johann Gottfried Herder. Smith employed the term 'American folk music', whereby he meant to include every kind of vernacular music that found its way to the United States. Like Herder, Smith was interested in pushing the boundaries of the world. In similar ways, his passion for the potential of recordings makes him also a cousin of Erich Moritz von Hornbostel. Smith was perhaps slightly less interested in what he was including in his anthology than in just being inclusive; his concern was to allow music to remap the cultural history and geography of the United States and to do so by dismantling the borders between American folk music and the world. Many discourses intersect in the *Anthology of American Folk Music*, but all are unified by the complex uses of recording. As an anthology, the project uses recording to make a record of recordings; the Smithsonian reissue adds yet another layer to the history of recording documented by the CDs, scholarly and anecdotal notes, and the reprint of Harry Smith's own 'handbook' for the recordings. Scholars and culture heroes alike contributed their voices to charting the musical field that the *Anthology* might possibly represent.

Throughout the 1980s and 1990s world music had slowly made inroads into the Grammy category for Best Historical Album. Blues (Robert Johnson in 1990) and jazz (Billie Holiday in 1991) anthologies had produced winning entries, and classical re-releases, though still dominating the nominations, were losing their grip on the award. What is so significant about the 1998 Grammy for the Smithsonian's reissue of Harry Smith's *Anthology* is that it employs the technological questions raised by recording and asks ethnomusicologists to rethink the relation of those questions to the spaces of ethnographic encounter and fieldwork. Recording itself seems at first to supplant the field, even as Harry Smith himself emerges from the booklets and liner notes as a spectator more than a theorist. He concerns himself with music for the record, and he insists that concern for making the record as complete as possible provides a common goal for all interested in world music. More critically, we might say that the Grammy was awarded not for the music but for the recording; more objectively, we might say that this is the nature of encountering and representing world music in the space between self and other.

Chapter 3
Between myth and history

The great leap forward – the 1932 Cairo Congress of Arab Music

For a month during the spring of 1932 Cairo, Egypt, became the epicentre for debates about the position of Arab music in world music. The brainchild of Maḥmūd Aḥmad al-Ḥifnī (1896–1973), the Congress of Arab Music gathered the greatest scholars and musicians from Europe and the best-known musicians from the Arab world, stretching from Morocco in the west to Iraq in the east. Al-Ḥifnī, who held the position of 'Inspector of Music' at the Egyptian Ministry of Education, enjoyed the strong backing of King Fu'ād and administrative assistance from the Academy of Oriental Music. The Congress would be a grand event, 'an East-West encounter', as Racy described it, on the highest musical and musicological plane. Years in planning and truly international in scope, it would recognize the enormous contribution of Arab music to the past history of world music and would lay the groundwork for an even greater contribution to the future. The Congress would embrace Arab music writ large in the annals of world music.

The goals of the 1932 Congress of Arab Music were ambitious and had all the trappings of an encounter that would change the course of world music history. The Europeans were brought to the Congress not only to witness the past but to provide expert advice for the proper path into the future. The list of musical and ethnomusicological dignitaries was indeed stellar, including the composers Paul Hindemith and Béla Bartók, orientalists such as Baron Carra de Vaux and Henry George Farmer, and ethnomusicologists such as Curt Sachs, Erich Moritz von Hornbostel, and Robert Lachmann. The delegations from North Africa and the Levant brought with them folk and art music ensembles, whose concerts would bear witness to the full support of governments from Morocco to Lebanon for the music culture of a nation entering the international community of nation-states. There were celebrities among the musicians as well, for example the Iraqi singer Muḥammad al-Qubbānjī, and, unknown to the participants, there were also a few would-be stars, notably Umm Kulthūm of Egypt, to whom we will turn shortly. The Congress indeed marked an auspicious moment for encounter in world music.

All did not turn out as expected, but perhaps that too should have been expected. More than anything, the Europeans and the Arab delegations brought with them quite different expectations about how Arab music would take its place in the future. We might have expected that the Europeans would argue for an historical agenda of change: wasn't it high time to untether Arab music from its past glories so that it could flourish again? Similarly, we might have expected the Arab delegations to use the event to showcase the past and to make a case for preserving it.

Just the opposite was the case. Recognizing the indebtedness of European music to the great traditions of North Africa and the eastern Mediterranean during the Middle Ages, the Europeans took a stance on the side of tradition. Tradition, however, meant that European and Arab music stood apart in world music history; it meant that they were different, but even more that they belonged to two distinctive historical epochs, one – Arab music – prior to modern history and the other – European music – coeval with modernity itself. The task of the Europeans as humanists, musicians, and ethnomusicologists was to respect and maintain that distinctiveness.

The Egyptians welcomed the gesture of respect, but it did not advance their cause, and it was not exactly the response for which they had been hoping. Whereas Arab pride in the greatness of the past was palpable in the themes of the Congress, the more visible agenda was modernity. How might the past serve as a springboard for the future? How might modern Western instruments be transformed for Arab music, say by retuning the piano for microtonal modal systems? How might recording and publishing projects be expanded, and how might they be used to disseminate Arab music to the world?

Clearly, the European and Arab delegations had two vastly different worlds in mind. For the Europeans it was the world of the past, a world in which Arab music had arguably been dominant, but also a world frozen at a great distance from the present. The European position bore all the earmarks of what Edward Said has called 'orientalism'. The orientalist 'East' was transformed by the European gaze into an object at which one might indeed marvel, but also an object that was helpless against the intervention of the West. The magnificence of Arab music, therefore, lay in its historical inertness, in the fact that its narrative had been closed.

The Arab delegations wanted to engage with world history anew, and they were unwilling to accept the orientalist arguments for historical closure. World music, as they wished to confront it, allowed change and was not irreconcilably stuck in the past. Behind their interest in change was the interaction between history and the nation-state. The government agencies in Egypt, from King Fu'ād on down, recognized that modern nation-states laid claim to national cultures, which played a role in shaping international dialogue. The nationalist agenda was clear also in the musical delegations, which represented 'nations' not 'cultures' or even 'traditions'. The musical delegations represented the national collective, for they arrived as ensembles, not as individuals, and they therefore reflected the polity of the modern nation-state.

In the history of world music during the 20th century, the 1932 Cairo Congress of Arab Music stands as a watershed, albeit one characterized by paradox. For many Arabic music scholars the Congress marks the moment at which Arab music history re-entered world music history, and the visibility of that moment is celebrated with publications and recording projects. The Congress, nonetheless, also serves as a reminder that what gets admitted to the canon of world music at any moment depends on government decisions as well as on commercial and scholarly decisions.

Mediating the medieval – North Africa in the history of world music

In the imagination of world history North Africa has long been the *locus classicus* of in-betweenness. Geographically, North Africa is connected by the Mediterranean to Europe, but separated from the rest of Africa by the Sahara. Historically, much that provided cultural foundations for Europe started in North Africa, for example the influence of ancient Egypt on Classical Greece and Rome. Theologically, Judaism, Christianity, and Islam all remained indebted to North Africa for extended periods of myth and mysticism. North Africa has also served as the border at which 'otherness' began, lying between that which Europe knew and all that was foreign to it. North Africa was the classic land of encounter, and it is hardly surprising that its role in the shaping of world music must be understood as the product of ongoing encounter.

In the Middle Ages it was North Africa not Europe that could claim dominance on the stage of world history and culture. Indeed, it was North African Islam rather than European Christianity that supported cultural advances – in science, in medicine, and in the arts – that were of truly global proportions from roughly the

9th century CE until the beginning of the Renaissance. The inventor of world history – historiography that took the world, in fact, the universe, as its subject – was North African, the great 14th-century polymath Ibn Khaldūn (1332–1406). Today, we know Ibn Khaldūn as a thinker and writer who was able to do it all. He was a diplomat whose posts took him from Spain to Damascus, so his travel accounts are rich ethnographies. He was a devout and mystical Muslim, or Sufi, hence his religious views are particularly revealing of Islam. He was a writer of history, who endeavoured in the 1370s to write a history of the universe, a task so sweeping that he was able only to complete the three volumes of the introduction, the *Muqaddimah* (the 'prolegomenon').

In the midst of all these activities he also turned his attention to music, indeed to world music. Viewed from the perspective of ethnomusicology today, Ibn Khaldūn actually appears to be very modern, even if we do not necessarily agree with all his findings. He wrote, for example, that different cultures had different musics, and he attributed this to, among other things, the impact of climate. He argued that music could influence human actions in profound ways, for example spurring men to go to war. Music exerted powerful influences, but it was nonetheless anchored in elaborate theoretical systems, with rules and structures that the scholar could perceive and understand. Still, as a Sufi, Ibn Khaldūn also recognized that there was much about music that humans could not understand, in other words, that its powers were also due to its sacredness. Music appears, throughout the *Muqaddimah*, inseparable from Ibn Khaldūn's view of world history itself.

Whatever its presence in the history of the world, the music of medieval North Africa was essential to the formation of the history of European music. Muslim theorists working in Arabic and Latin, such as al-Fārābī and Ibn Sīnā (better known by his Latin name, Avicenna), wrote works seminal to the thinking about music in Europe's Christian monasteries. So powerful was the influence of North Africa on music and the science of music that later generations took it for granted and overlooked the presence of Arabic music in European music. Take the instrument of measurement in Arab music theory, the *'ūd*, whose strings allowed theorists to determine the structures of scales and explain the physics of sound, all the while demonstrating many of the auditory traits closest to the human voice. We can trace that instrument from the eastern Mediterranean, where its name, *al-'ūd* (the wood) followed it across North Africa with Islam to the Iberian peninsula, where it was altered in Spanish and Portuguese to forms of *la-ute*, which then underwent further modification to *Laute* in Germanic languages and 'lute' in English.

As a land of in-betweenness North Africa was not a single music culture but many, and the confluence of musics that these effected was also significant for the region's position in world music. In addition to the presence of classical Arab musics, which produced both instrumental and vocal canons, North Africa was a home to countless dialects and hybrids of vernacular music, that is, folk music. The music of the Berbers, for example, was vastly different from the Arab classical traditions. The nomadic peoples of the region, such as the Bedouins, have long possessed rich narrative traditions of their own, not least among them the great *hilali* epic cycles. In the western parts of North Africa (the 'Maghreb' in a westernized form of the Arabic distinction), Islamic musics mixed with Christian and Jewish traditions, producing one of the greatest of all hybrid classical traditions, Andalusian music. In the wake of the *reconquista*, which led to the expulsion of Jews and Muslims from Spain and Portugal in the 1490s, North Africa quickly gave rise to new classical and hybrid traditions, especially that of the Sephardic Jews, whose vernacular language, *ladino*, was a linguistic offshoot of Spanish.

If North Africa was positioned at Europe's periphery, many European scholars did not lose sight of the fact that they might discover remnants – even whole pieces – of their own past there. As European thought began to open toward the world during the Age of Discovery, North Africa was close at hand, and accordingly the musical thinkers of Early Modern Europe turned to the region as a laboratory. North Africa may have been a world of otherness, but it was not entirely strange. One did not have to train the Early Modern gaze on too fine an object before it suggested that the object might further serve as a lens to Europe's past, and then beyond Europe's past to the beginnings of music itself in the eastern Mediterranean. The music of North Africa could not be dismissed from the growing interest in world histories of music; indeed, the music of North Africa made such histories possible.

The encounter with Islam, North Africa, and the Middle East is everywhere in European music from the 18th century to the present, so much so that again we sometimes overlook the possibility that there might not be a Western music without this music of the 'other'. Whether in opera libretti from Mozart to Verdi or in the wind and percussion sections of the modern orchestra, Western music has gathered elements of the Islamic world as if to strip them of their differences. Difference, however, was not stripped away, and for these reasons some musical scholars took it upon themselves to figure out just what it was that North Africa had given to Europe. The musical scholar Guillaume-André Villoteau, for example, accompanied the scientific team that Napoleon packed off to Egypt, later publishing two encyclopedic volumes on the music of the region. As Europe intensified its colonialist interventions across the Mediterranean, musical scholars were there, gathering and systematizing more evidence that would allow them to cast the music of the 'other' as their own. Scholars and writers of all kinds turned their gaze toward North Africa, often leaving us with some of the most penetrating descriptions of music, for example in the novels of Gustave Flaubert and in the stories of Paul Bowles. The in-betweenness of the music of North Africa did not escape them, above all because they themselves were critical factors in the calculus of that in-betweenness.

Umm Kulthūm – a star is born

There are those who would say that Umm Kulthūm (1904–75) was
the most popular singer of the 20th century. Statistically, it would
be hard to refute such claims. Umm Kulthūm enjoyed success as a
recording artist, making an estimated 300 recordings in her
lifetime. It is surely the case that wherever one goes to purchase
recordings in the Islamic world – the marketplace of North African
towns, CD shops in the Muslim neighbourhoods of New York,
London, or Paris, or in airport electronic shops in Pakistan or
Indonesia – there will be a surfeit of Umm Kulthūm recordings.
During the last part of her career in Egypt, moreover, Umm
Kulthūm was perhaps best known for her radio and television
broadcasts, which together constitute something of a national myth
about the country coming to a halt when Umm Kulthūm's voice was
heard. In films with and about Umm Kulthūm her status as an
icon – as a woman, a musician, and an Egyptian – came to convey
its meanings beyond Egyptian society to world music. Umm
Kulthūm's fame and the dissemination of her music not only
outlived her but have risen with the media of worldbeat and have
profited from the myth-making of post-colonialism.

Umm Kulthūm's stardom and her iconic presence in world music
are not without paradox. Her life as a singer was in many ways
traditional. She came rather early in life to singing, albeit within a
strictly Muslim context. Her father was the local *imam*, or the
leader of the village mosque, and at the age of five she began to
attend the village religious school. It was here that learning was
based on audible recitation of the Qur'an, which meant learning the
rules of recitation. It was not long before Umm Kulthūm could join
her father at weddings and other religious festivities, where he sang
semi-professionally. This was how she learned to sing and how she
acquired a repertory of sacred song.

In every respect traditional song provided the basis for Umm
Kulthūm's style and repertory for the rest of her life. We might ask,

then, whether she became a famous singer on the stage of world music despite the role and restrictions of tradition. The ways in which she employed mode, or *maqām*, were anchored in the recitation of the Qur'an. Prosody and poetic patterns owed their form and function to sacred texts. Even the relation of her voice to the ensembles accompanying her, small orchestras during the last decades of her life, revealed her unwillingness to abandon fundamental Muslim aesthetics.

The distinguished scholar and biographer of Umm Kulthūm, Virginia Danielson, provides us with a forceful counterargument, namely that it was because of the contexts of tradition and her reticence to violate them that Umm Kulthūm became a figure of international proportions. Danielson writes that 'to be a listener to Umm Kulthūm was to join many others in a validation of a communal social universe'. The world that Umm Kulthūm's songs evoked was, therefore, not primarily global but local, and though it assumed many different forms and meanings, it was palpable and personal in the lives of listeners throughout the world. It was at once both individual and shared. It both substantiated the aesthetic resonance of sacred song in the present and carved out new political and ideological potential for tradition in a changing world. In so doing she occupied a crucial place on the stage of world music, transforming the ways it gave voice to women and the popular ethos of modern Egypt and the Muslim world.

Islam and the meaning of music

Were we to have been flies on the wall at the 1932 Cairo Congress, listening to the various Arab delegations debating their agendas, to the Europeans trying to find a common scientific language, and to Umm Kulthūm conversing with her instrumentalists about which songs would best represent their tradition, we probably would have wondered if they were all talking about the same thing. It would not only have been a matter that different terms were applied to the same subject, but that some terms were avoided or used with a studied obliqueness. Umm Kulthūm, very likely, would not have referred to her singing as 'music', a term she would have reserved only for the instrumental ensemble accompanying her. If the Europeans had pressed the Arab musicians to provide practical examples of theoretical concepts, the musicians might well have played something out of politeness, but they would have wondered what the foreigners meant by confusing theory and practice. We were not flies on the walls at the Cairo Congress, of course, but we do know that the Congress, the historic character of its encounter notwithstanding, produced little agreement on anything. In part, such results are endemic to encounter. In part, they were inevitable in Cairo in 1932 because of the complex ways in which it is possible to talk about music within Islam – or more to the point, not to talk about music.

Complicating the discourse about music in North Africa and the eastern Mediterranean are the questions arising from Islamic attitudes toward music. These attitudes range from contentions that Islam condemns music altogether to judgements that Islamic writings are at best ambivalent toward its practice. Two primary literary sources are traditionally used to justify the interpretation of music's acceptability: the Qur'an and the many interpretive works concerning the Prophet Mohammad's teachings, called *aḥādīth* (commentaries). Neither source is unequivocal in its pronouncements concerning music. The Qur'an contains *surat* (chapters) that seem to condone activities associated with music, as well as *surat* cited as evidence that Mohammad condemned music. Even these primary writings, however, do not address music per se but rather cultural activities with which music might be associated, such as poetry or dance. There is relatively little detailed discussion of the arts by the earliest theologians of Islam. The early Islamic writings that do include discussions of the arts seldom offer any doctrine that might be called a theory of aesthetics. It is hardly surprising, therefore, that modern positions toward music (e.g. prohibition under the former Taliban regime in Afghanistan) vary greatly. We read early writings that refer to music only circumstantially, together with pre-Islamic beliefs and social phenomena that Islam does not condone. The *aḥādīth* also frequently originated in lands conquered during the spread of Islam, and they therefore initially referred to the cultural activities therein in very specifically didactic ways. As Islam spread across North Africa, music was extrinsic rather than intrinsic to its concerns.

In the course of Arab music history musical terminology increasingly framed the articulation of distinctions between what was inside and outside Muslim society, and what was acceptable and questionable. Recitation of the Qur'an (*qirā'ah*) and the call to prayer (*adhān*) were not considered musical activities at all, but rather practices designated as 'reading', one of the literal meanings of *qirā'ah*. The role of music in the reading of religious texts is that of enhancing the meaning through clarification. It is this role that provided the basis of Umm Kulthūm's 'musical' education. What to the Western observer sounds like music is unquestionably secondary to matters of textual projection and religious expression within Muslim contexts. In North Africa, then, genres of strictly vocal music are greeted with greater favour than are genres employing instruments.

Once attention turns to the meanings associated with instrumental genres the terminology of musical discourse suddenly bears witness to foreign concepts, to an otherness within Islam itself. One encounters, for example, the widespread use of the term *mūsīqā* (or *mūsīqī*), borrowed from the Greek language. Properly used, *mūsīqā* could never apply to *qirā'ah* or *adhān*. Among the Islamic sciences that flourished in the Middle Ages, *mūsīqā* designated the presence of foreignness, serving as an unequivocal marker of cultural distance. Terminological distinctions were used to calibrate that cultural distance, as in describing secular music that is strictly vocal as *ghinā'* (song), thus stripping it of possible associations with instruments. When Ibn Khaldūn wrote about song and instrumental music in the *Muqaddimah*, for example, he did so in entirely different sections of his prolegomenon, dispelling any notion that they were related. It was hardly surprising in the 20th century that the delegations at the Cairo Congress found themselves talking about such vastly different phenomena. Such distinctions were even greater in modern colonial contexts, where the Western 'music' had acquired many of the same associations with foreignness or instrumental music (for example in India). From an Islamic perspective such differences are prerequisites for talking about world music at all.

The gaze of ethnomusicology – Robert Lachmann in North Africa

The 1932 Cairo Congress was not the first orientalist excursion into North Africa for all the participants. Robert Lachmann (1890–1939), a senior music librarian for the Berlin Prussian State Library and editor of the most prestigious German-language journal in comparative musicology, had made several research trips to the Maghreb in the 1920s. It was because of this experience that he was chosen to serve as the official reporter for the European musicians, composers, and scholars visiting the Cairo Congress.

During the course of his ethnomusicological trips Lachmann changed his understanding of the musical world of the Maghreb. When he first visited North Africa in the 1920s, Lachmann imagined himself taking a journey into Europe's past. He believed he would find traces of music that had not changed for centuries, and he thought that, if his ethnographic time travels took him far enough from the modern and urban world of the northern Mediterranean, he might be able to document the prehistory of European music.

What Robert Lachmann expected to find and what he found were two different historical phenomena. During one of his more extended field trips to Tunisia, Lachmann made the decision to focus on the old Jewish communities on the island of Djerba, located in the Mediterranean Sea off the coast of Tunisia. Djerba had all the trappings of an 'isolated' music culture, and for a comparative musicologist in the 1920s it seemed like the ideal laboratory. Because of the great age of the Jewish communities, really no more than two villages with several hundred souls each, Djerba might also add considerable evidence to the theories A. Z. Idelsohn and other Jewish music scholars were developing about the preservation of music from before the time of the destruction of the second temple in Jerusalem (70 CE). It would not be so much a 'missing link' as the introductory chapter in the music history from Antiquity to the present.

The music Robert Lachmann collected on Djerba, however, left little doubt that it was more modern than ancient. First of all, though most of the sacred music, such as that in the synagogues of the Djerba villages, was clearly Jewish because of texts in Hebrew and ritual functions, it nonetheless sounded like the music of Muslim villages in Djerba and elsewhere in Tunisia. Second, the instruments and modal structures of much secular music were indistinguishable from other Maghrebi styles. Third, the music of Djerba's Jewish women was virtually indistinguishable from Muslim vernacular repertories. It would be impossible for Lachmann to claim that Djerba's music had remained 'Jewish' and that it survived in the isolation of an island off the North African coast.

Robert Lachmann was not deterred, and he asked how the conditions leading to hybridity might have come about. By listening carefully to the music and analysing it, he found his answers. Djerba, though geographically isolated, was on an important pilgrimage route across North Africa to the eastern Mediterranean. Jewish and Muslim pilgrims sojourned on the island, and when they departed, they also left traces of their music, some of which were integrated into the local music. Even more significantly, Jews, Muslims, and others on Djerba and the Tunisian mainland obviously shared a common musical life, and exchange was more often the rule than the exception. Djerba's Jewish music was not the vestige of an ancient past but evidence for a vital present.

The last decade of Robert Lachmann's life was marked by many of the tragedies that befell German-Jewish intellectuals. When the Nazis assumed power in Germany in 1933, he was dismissed from his librarian's post, and he was denied any possible future in Hitler's Germany. Because of his activities as a scholar and editor – and also because of the international contacts that followed from his important role at the 1932 Cairo Congress – Lachmann was able to gain support from the young Hebrew University for moving his archives and ethnomusicological laboratory to Jerusalem, where he was able to lay the foundations for modern Israeli musicology. In his publications and in the public lectures he delivered before his untimely death in 1939, Lachmann portrayed the musical worlds of North Africa and the eastern Mediterranean as modern, even multicultural, where change and response to contemporary conditions produced a hybridity that earlier generations of ethnomusicologists would not have dared to imagine. The music of North Africa proved not to be primarily a link to the past; rather, it was the Cairo Congress and Lachmann's Djerba research that formed a link to the present.

Raï and the mediation of millennia

The popular music of North Africa exists precariously in the fissures of post-colonial, postmodern in-betweenness. Popular musicians sing against the institutions of the politically powerful, yet depend upon the connections of such institutions to the former colonizing nations, especially the recording industries of Paris and London. Popular music mobilizes the voiceless, but when the voiceless turn to Islam to enhance their mobilization, they cannot at the same time embrace popular music. Popular music enters the North African metropolis from the peripheries of tradition, but must sacrifice the past to enter the public sphere at the centre of urban society. Paradox is everywhere – in the social contexts and the poetic texts of popular music – and it is precisely because of that paradox that popular music so powerfully connects centuries-long tradition to the most recent currents of world music.

No other North African popular music has secured a place as palpably in the postmodern imagination as has *raï*, which means something like 'a way of seeing' or 'an opinion'. *Raï* is the music of the urban disenfranchised in North Africa, especially in Algeria and eastern Morocco. It is a music whose roots and early parameters are in many ways very specific. During the colonial era, when France dominated the Maghreb, *raï* emerged as the music of the subcultures between the rural and the urban. *Raï* musicians performed at the margins of the cities (especially of Oran, Algeria's second largest city), where its venues were socially and economically marginal. The musicians were a mixed lot, and there were more than a few musicians who would not have been sanctioned by orthodox Islam to sing in public, especially women but also musicians from ethnic and religious minorities.

Because of this marginal position *raï* flourished as a music determined by hybridity. Its texts were largely in dialect, thus contrasting with classical Arabic or the élite use of French in the cities. Typically, the texts depended on complex layers of meaning, with the political and the sexual inextricably bound together. Musically, *raï* drew wantonly from every conceivable style: Maghrebi classical and semi-classical music; Western, especially Mediterranean and French, popular styles, such as the *chanson*; Arabic popular styles, such as *qasīda* and *layālī*, familiar across North Africa by virtue of Umm Kulthūm; bands with traditional Arabic instruments and those with a highly electrified sound.

Raï depends for its survival as a world music – and for the survival of its singers, many of whose lives are at risk in Algeria – on the ability to juxtapose contrasting meanings and to express a significance that every segment of post-colonial North Africa can perceive as its own. To some degree we might understand this capacity as inherent in *raï*'s traditionality. It reflects the ambiguity toward music that we found in Islamic aesthetic tenets; the meaning of text is privileged, with instrumental accompaniment being secondary; its poetics depend entirely on the Arabic language, particularly Maghrebi dialects. The rise of *raï*, Marc Schade-Poulsen suggests, has paralleled the rise of Islam in Algeria, as if the music fulfils the same political ends in the post-colonial struggle as does Islamic fundamentalism.

We might also interpret the attraction of *raï* as stereotypically orientalist. Its traditional settings in social clubs are seldom distanced from the open expression of sexuality; texts are as openly nostalgic as they are politically empowering; as world music *raï* evokes the marketplace of the Muslim city, the harem, the court, and the social gathering where forbidden substances are used. When the producers of the 1997 science-fiction movie *The Fifth Element* needed a soundtrack to accompany Bruce Willis as he raced through the confused fantasy of the futuristic metropolis, a song by perhaps the most famous *raï* star, Khaled, fitted the bill. The jumble that *raï* has absorbed becomes the East writ large. In the mediated world imagined through worldbeat, the producers of *raï* have succumbed to the allure of full-blown orientalism.

And what about the singers and musicians? What about the audiences and those for whom the message, in the subtle poetic voice of their own dialect, still has meaning? Have they been left behind by *raï*'s meteoric rise to the stage of world music? Yes and no. That *raï* continues to speak to the post-colonial politics of North Africa could not be clearer than in the Algerian suburbs and neighbourhoods of Paris, where the stars of *raï* find their old audiences again. Literally and figuratively, the music remains at the margins, but for the thousands who fill stadiums for concerts or listen intently to the lyrics that speak of exile and the irretrievability of the past, *raï* remains intensely personal. It embodies the Algeria that struggles to secure a position in a post-colonial world. *Raï* remains real and its message poignant.

The popular musicians of modern North Africa and the eastern Mediterranean have responded to their position in world music with what we might even call a traditional ambivalence. There seems to be little evidence, for example, that Umm Kulthūm or Khaled and other *raï* singers ever rejected Western instruments, or, for that matter, the inevitable challenges to harmonic structure, form, and public presence that Western instruments generate. There are also few instances in which the stars of North African popular music simply left their traditions behind to be managed and manipulated by record producers and tour organizers. Finally, these popular musicians did not avoid encounter, for their music and the meanings so crucial to their public presence depended also on how they mediated the encounter between tradition and modernity. Their sense of selfness was empowered by the insatiable hunger for otherness in world music.

Chapter 4
Music of the folk

Béla Bartók and the women who stayed home

In Budapest, that most urbane of former imperial metropolises in East-Central Europe, folk music has always enjoyed pride of place. So it was during the centuries when the Hungarian king shared power with the Austrian emperor to form the Austro-Hungarian Empire; so it was during the waning years of the Cold War when Hungary experimented with a liberal form of communism; and so it is during the era of the New Europe as Hungary unabashedly responds to the seduction of a globalized economy. Hungarians, from aesthetic ideologues to folk music scholars and ethnomusicologists to cultural marketing specialists, have located folk music on the historical fast track from the periphery to the centre, from the ritual of the village to the culture of the capital, and from the narrative journey of myth to history.

As Budapest bolstered itself for the onslaught of cultural tourists in the summer of 2001, it was hardly surprising that folk music would again define the centre through its representation of the periphery. The centre was the castle grounds of Buda, with its command of the Danube and the shopping districts of Pest, spreading out along the flood plain of the Danube. Opening the 'Budapest Summer Night Performances' of 2001 was a troupe that had long gathered, presented, and revived the folk music of Hungary, the 'Honvéd

Dance Theatre', literally the 'Army' Dance Theatre. The connection of the 'Honvéd' ensemble to the army was its name, for the singers and dancers did not really serve in the army. The question remained, nonetheless, whether this connection or lack thereof was real or virtual. The featured soloist of the opening performance in the Military History Museum sector of the castle grounds was Katalin Szvorák, the recipient in 2000 of the prestigious Franz Liszt Prize for musical excellence, whose musical training during the 1980s had taken place almost entirely in the army, where she and others in the Honvéd troupes of the time performed in folk choruses and orchestras.

Prior to 1989, these folk musicians performed together in theatres and on television, drawing upon repertories from cultural districts within Hungary and in the Hungarian-speaking regions of Hungary's neighbours, especially Romania, (then) Czechoslovakia, and (then) Yugoslavia. The official folk music of the 1980s was music with a message, above all an historical message about the displacement of national peoples and boundaries, and the power of folk music to effect their replacement at the centre of the cultural orbit generated from Budapest.

In 2001 the Honvéd Dance Theatre was no less engaged in using folk music to represent the displacement and replacement of borders. The work chosen for its 'Budapest Summer' performance bore the title 'Wedding', a choreographed representation of a village wedding by Jolan Foltin and Ferenc Kiss, which was itself award-winning. 'Wedding' relied on folk song and folk dance for its primary materials, which wore their authenticity so all could hear and see it. Music, dance, and costumes all came from the Hungarian-speaking communities around Nitra, in western Slovakia. The narrative of the performance proved to tug at the edges of authenticity, especially at the beginning and end when an electronic soundtrack, with New Age reverb, framed the entrance into and exit from the dream sequences in the stylized ritual of the wedding itself. Once the dream was entered, authenticity captured the ritual as its own, for it was at the core of the performance that Katalin Szvorák and the Hegedös Ensemble provided the music and the Honvéd troupe danced out the ritual of a Hungarian wedding in rural Slovakia.

The pride of place that folk music enjoys in Hungary is only possible because of the extensive investment of symbolic capital in folk music. Folk musicians acquire national prominence, and as that prominence increases, so too does the potential export capital that it might bring. In the 1990s, Hungarian musicians paved their way into worldbeat with folk music, usually a dual repertory of centralized Hungarian repertories with traditions from the historical and geographic peripheries to destabilize and relocate the otherwise parochial borders. Even the most successful Hungarian worldbeat stars, the group 'Muzsikás' and its singer Márta Sebestyén, stuck close to Hungarian folk music, ever so slightly experimenting with styles just across the borders still identifiable as Hungarian (e.g. *The Lost Jewish Musicians of Transylvania*).

The scholars of Hungarian folk music, too, have acquired the status of national culture heroes. In the first half of the 20th century the composers Béla Bartók (1881–1945) and Zoltán Kodály (1882–1967) were known as ethnomusicologists *and* composers, whereby their nationalism and modernism were welded into a single cultural identity. Bartók and Kodály were neither the first nor last Hungarian composers to take an active and activist interest in folk music. Franz Liszt, who otherwise lived almost not at all in Hungary, penned an influential book about the impact of Rom (Gypsy) music on the Western tradition. Folk music embodied and grew from a musical discourse of Hungarianness, and the stakes of that discourse were very high indeed, for they raised questions not only of ethnic identity but of racial purity and of national integrity.

When Bartók is portrayed among the pantheon – usually at the centre of that pantheon – of great Hungarian musicians, it is almost

6. Béla Bartók collecting folk songs in a Slovak village (1907)

7. Béla Bartók with gramophone

inevitably with one of two photographs (Figures 6 and 7). In the first, we witness Bartók accompanied by his cylinder recorder in a Slovak village, with a line of peasants waiting to sing for him. In the second, Bartók sits at his desk, this time with his ear turned toward the recording horn of a gramophone. Folk songs entered one recording horn, and they issued from the other, finding their way through Bartók's minuscule and detailed transcriptions to the anthologies of the Hungarian folk music canon and the compositions of Hungarian modernism. The two recording horns symbolize the modernity of authenticity, but they make even clearer the intervention of ideology at the expense of authenticity. The stages of mediation could not be more evident. Song emanates from the women who had never left the village and who therefore knew nothing other than authenticity. At the national centre, in the urbane culture of a modern Hungary, the authentic was recovered, but only after a chain of representations. Paradoxically, it was at the centre that the world of the village was fully realized, where the cultural institutions of the modern nation-state could breathe new life into it.

The performance of Foltin and Kiss's 'Wedding' for the 'Budapest Summer Night Performances' during June 2001 appeared, at first glance, to typify the tourist fare usually served up at such open-air events. It would have been hard to know, however, how tourists might have responded, for ultimately nothing was done to make the performance 'tourist-friendly': no explanation in a language other than Hungarian, no translations, indeed, no printed texts of any kind. And there was no attempt to explain why the 'especially authentic and beautiful' traditions of Hungarian villages in Slovakia continued to be historically relevant in Budapest at the beginning of the 21st century. There was no need to do any of this because it was not lost upon anyone in the crowd that folk music and dance had lost none of their power to reinscribe history on the face of the New Hungary performed within the very bastions of the Old Hungary.

Folk music in the transformation from myth to history

To Big Bill Broonzy is attributed one of the most frequently cited yet dismissive of all explanations of folk song: 'I guess all songs is folksongs, never heard no horse sing 'em'. A definition by way of avoiding definitions. A recognition of the universal at the level of the personal. Folk song and folk music are everywhere and potentially owned by everyone, as if they were so commonplace as to defy any further discussion. They are anachronistic, connected primarily to a previous era, but they live in the present, shaped by and responsive to contemporary events. Still, we wonder, if horses don't sing folk songs, who does? If Bill Broonzy had it right, that 'all songs is folksongs', he kept rather selective company, for most of us, in fact, do not hear those around us singing folk songs with any frequency.

Arguably, folk song and folk music constitute the original world music, the mother lode in an historical tradition of connecting music to global phenomena. The discourse about folk music derives from an impulse to imagine world music. When Johann Gottfried Herder, writing from the heart of the Enlightenment, coined the term *Volkslied* (folk song), he deliberately documented it with examples from throughout the world as he knew it. He included songs collected by missionaries in colonial Latin America, juxtaposing these with poetry from Shakespeare and Goethe. Herder's folk songs possessed national attributes, and they both shored up and transgressed linguistic borders. Less succinct than Bill Broonzy, Herder nonetheless imagined a distribution of folk song as world music that was equally as capacious and generous.

If folk music made it possible to imagine the world musically, it did so according to a particularly European perspective. When European scholars, embracing Herder's seminal writings, identified folk music beyond Europe's borders, it more often than not resembled European folk music. Mobility was one of the most frequent attributes of folk music, empowering scholars to scour the globe for variants that had accompanied the migrations of entire peoples. At the same time, mapping the world with folk music had all the earmarks of colonialism, and it was hardly by chance that concepts of folk music were also rallied to justify European expansion. If the collection of folk music was implicated in European encounters throughout the world, folk music came increasingly to reflect the ideologies of modernity, not just colonialism but also nationalism and the fundamentalist search for authenticity. Folk music attracted the political left no less than the political right; it became an emblem of modernity and provided a vocabulary for its malcontents.

How did folk music become the first world music? To answer this question would require one to be as elusive as those who define folk music by avoiding real definitions. For want of a definition it is necessary to consider the ways in which folk music has been a metaphor, indeed, a field of metaphors, that has consistently connected music to the world and connected different parts of the world through music. The metaphor of folk music as 'connection' can be particularly helpful. In many traditional senses, folk music occupies a cultural space in which music forms the synapses that make connection possible.

The cultural space of folk music responds to two broadly conceived sets of metaphors, the first temporal and the second spatial. By their very nature, the temporal and the spatial metaphors of folk music's cultural space are mutually dependent. Folk music's temporal spaces are made possible because of its numerous *narrative* qualities, in other words, the capacity of folk music to tell stories. These stories may be tales about individuals or communities, and they may generalize the moments that together form the narrative of human life. They employ fantasy to make characters and events larger than life, or they may take specific historical occurrences as points of departure. There are repertories of folk songs that function in tandem with rites of passage, and there are others that, removed generations from historical events, create a narrative space for the past to live in the present. As different as these narrative qualities are, they transform folk song and dance into stages on which the complex events that define a community, region, or nation are performed.

By invoking the metaphor of the stage, it is clear already that the temporal and spatial metaphors of folk music are interdependent. The narrative qualities of folk music are, nonetheless, distinct from the *geographical* qualities. In many different ways folk music proclaims rather loudly that it is about place. Song texts identify the place in which they take place, usually in the first line or two, and dance forms use movement to outline the place from which they come or in which they take place. The quintessential rural Alpine folk dance, the *Ländler*, not only comes from the *Land* – 'land' has many geographical meanings, however in the *Ländler* it is Alpine cultural geography – but in its original forms makes it possible for dancers to act out with dance 'figures', or stylized gestures, their relationship to life in the mountains of Central Europe. The dancers of the Hungarian Honvéd Dance Theatre and Katalin Szvorák represented the spaces of a Hungarian-speaking village in Slovakia in the region of Nitra, not just any place where a traditional wedding might have occurred.

By specifying place, narrative and history were also specified, as were their political and nationalistic meaning in the present. The intersection of narrative and geographical qualities made it possible to use the cultural space of folk music to make claims on that space and thus to make a case for ownership. Folk music's narrative and geographical qualities coalesce in such ways that they allow a collective metaphorically to enter, through performance, the cultural spaces evoked, opened, and then represented by folk music. Bartók realized this when he collected folk songs from the Hungarian regions of Romania and Slovakia no less than the Honvéd Dance Theatre. So, too, did the generations of German scholars who mapped the 'folk-song landscapes' of so-called *Sprachinseln* (speech islands), thereby also mapping potential routes for the expansion of German control over most of Europe in the world wars of the 20th century.

The cultural spaces of European folk music are and have been ceaselessly contested, often within the text of a single song or dance. Real and imagined spaces appear, and the characters of the song struggle to occupy the spaces, metaphorically representing the many different levels at which the struggle for place and history are carried out. We might take as an example the Yiddish folk ballad 'Hinter Poilen Wohnt a Yid'. Even at the most local levels the narrative and geographical qualities of the song reveal a struggle for space. The daughter in an observant Jewish family challenges her parents as well as her community by asking to enter the public spaces beyond traditional community life. Both her parents and European history deny access to that public space. It was not until the mid-19th century that European Jews were permitted to own land of their own. The more local issue, especially in this version of a folk ballad with non-Jewish variants (e.g. in the first canon of German folk poetry, *Des Knaben Wunderhorn*, and in a setting by Johannes Brahms), is the requirement imposed on the young woman by her suitor, a scribe, thus one who tells the stories of and for others, that she convert if she is to remain in the public sphere as his wife. Few variants of the folk song resolve the dilemma posed by this conflict between real and unrealizable spaces; in many, the Jewish girl chooses suicide rather than conversion, throwing herself into the sea. The powerful metaphors in 'Die Jüdin' were hardly lost upon the Yiddish folk song revival of the 1980s and 1990s, when European folk singers sought again to create a space for Jewish culture in Europe after the Holocaust. Jewish folk songs could not retrieve or remake those spaces, but their narrative power could make them more difficult to eliminate from the history of European modernity.

'Hinter Poilen Wohnt a Yid' [On the Other Side of Poland There Lived a Jew]

On the other side of Poland there lived a Jew
With a marvelous wife;
Her hair was beautifully braided,
Just as she was beautifully made-up;
And she danced wonderfully.

Mother, dearest mother,
I have such a headache;
Let me go for a little while
For a walk on the street!

Daughter, dearest daughter,
You cannot go alone;
Take your youngest sister,
You can go with her!

Mother, dearest mother,
My sister is a young child;
She'll rip up the flowers,
That are growing along the street!

Mother, you dearest mother,
I have such a headache;
Let me go for a little while
For a walk on the street!

Daughter, dearest daughter,
You cannot go alone;
Take your youngest brother,
You can go with him!

Mother, dearest mother,
My brother is a young child;
He'll rip up the flowers,
Which would be a terrible shame!

The mother went to bed,
The daughter jumped from the window;
She jumped over the iron fence,
Where the scribe was waiting for her.

Scribe, you dearest,
Scribe, you who are mine,
How can that be possible?
– If you let yourself be baptized,
You'll be called Mary Magdalene
And you'll be my wife!

Leadbelly and the making of a folk musician

> This was indeed a children's music; this was a people's music; this was folk music.
>
> > Moses Asch describing a 1940s Leadbelly concert at the
> > Metropolitan Museum of Art in New York City
> > (Asch and Lomax, 1962: 6)

No folk musician did more to raise the profile of folk song in America during the first half of the 20th century than did Huddie Ledbetter, generally known as Leadbelly (1885–1949). Leadbelly became an icon of what folk music had been prior to modernization, in the African-American culture of the 19th-century South, and for what it would become once discovered by collectors, scholars, and record companies. Born in rural Louisiana, Leadbelly acquired his musical skills early in life, picking up the 12-string guitar he used to accompany a repertory that he himself numbered at some 500 songs. As a young man, he rambled between jobs in Louisiana and Texas, between the cotton fields and the booming oil fields, if we are to believe the apocryphal stories that consistently portray Leadbelly plying the boundaries between an anachronistic past and an oppressive present. He also served time in various prisons, not just for misdemeanours, rather also for several serious felonies, among them murder (1918–25) and attempted murder (1930–4). It was while serving time for the second of these felonies in the Louisiana State Penitentiary that John Lomax 'discovered' Leadbelly, a fully-fledged blues singer, ripe for picking and presenting to the Library of Congress.

There can be no question that Leadbelly played a crucial role in the transformation of African-American folk music to world music, not only during the 15 years of his public career in the mid-20th century, but in the subsequent generations of folk music revival throughout the world. As his two names seemed to symbolize, Leadbelly shifted between several identities. As 'Leadbelly' he could sing and play the blues, as well as Southern folk songs and dances from a variety of genres. As Leadbelly he attracted the attention of scholars – not just the Lomaxes (discussed below) and Seegers (see Chapter 1), but ethnomusicologists such as George Herzog at Columbia University – and record producers, notably Moses Asch at Folkways Records and Folkways Music Publishers. 'Huddie Ledbetter' was both more ancient and more modern than Leadbelly, signally both a deep-rooted connection to rural Southern songs in oral tradition and the official name he used as singer-songwriter-composer of a prodigious number of songs (e.g. 'Rock Island Line', 'Midnight Special', 'House of the Rising Sun', and 'Good Night Irene') that became hits in their day and anthems for revivals in the decades to come. Disentangling myth from history in Leadbelly's biography is quite impossible.

Why would we, however, need to disentangle myth from history? That the 'folk music' Leadbelly performed both was myth and was invented to serve as myth goes without saying. As a consummate performer, who relished the various roles he was asked to assume, Leadbelly recognized the power of folk music to navigate the blurred borderlands between myth and history. He recognized that his anachronistic blues style might appeal the most to northern white liberals, but that a more eclectic fusion of black song styles might win him audiences in New York City jazz clubs. With his music he could evoke and even reify a panoply of cultural spaces, some representing moments in his own life, the Great Migration, the Great Depression, and World War II. He could talk with and through those who recognized his potential as maker of myths and chronicler of history, thus he allowed the Lomaxes and the Seegers and the folk music revival to imagine the myths for which he could serve as an icon. Whatever the mix of myth and history in Leadbelly's life, folk music won a much greater place in both because of that life.

Celtic music and the regional cartography of folk music

How does folk music become world music? Does it lose its attributes as folk music once it circulates globally? Perhaps no other music yields answers to these questions more directly than Celtic music. There are few places in the world, within and without the world music scene, where Celtic music has not made its presence known. It is hard to imagine a metropolis anywhere in the world that does not have at least one pub or tavern hosting live Celtic music; in large cities such as Vienna, Sydney, and Tokyo, one can pick and choose from a surfeit of Celtic offerings almost every night. Celtic music is a staple of world music festivals, and Celtic music festivals have enjoyed almost unchecked proliferation in the past decade. The phenomenal success of Celtic music, nonetheless, has depended on its ability to retain its folk roots.

Myth and history intersect in Celtic music, so much so that it has been myth that has the most direct historical path to world music. In its global forms as world music, Celtic music relies on the myths it narrates about itself. Myth, we might say, is very modern, and as such it follows from the ways in which the histories of Celtic music have been constructed. The myths of Celtic music take shape in the distant past. Supported by a long scientific tradition of archaeology, scholars have long thought of the Celts as a Bronze-Age culture that spread across the whole of Europe; they were proto-European Europeans, a fact derived from antiquity that bolsters the claims of modernity. As the Romans pushed northward and then various Asian peoples pushed westward into Europe during the first centuries of the Common Era, Celtic tribes initially offered stiff resistance and then retreated to the northern and western fringes of Europe, lands that remained Celtic and, by extension, autochthonously European until the present.

Histories of Celtic peoples and lands stress their unity, a unity that has acquired mythical proportions. Language is one of the most frequently extolled myths of unity, which also finds its way into the modern myths of Celtic music. The two major Celtic-language families, the Goidelic and the Brythonic, bear witness to cultural survival, the ability of native speakers to maintain them, clinging to them and thus to the earlier era from which they presumably have come. Religion, too, has mixed myth and history to underscore unity, for 'Celtic religion' has acquired a double meaning, on one hand, a pagan, pre-Christian past, preserved archaeologically in the stone evidence for cultic practices, and on the other, the historical practices of Christianity, which followed distinctive musical routes in the Middle Ages. The modern histories of resistance to English dominance (in Ireland and the British Isles) and French dominance (in Brittany) contribute further to the construction of myths that unify the Celtic fringe (see Map 1), myths whose dimensions have spread through the formation of a Celtic diaspora over the course of several centuries as Irish, Bretons, or Welsh were forced to emigrate because of inhospitable political and economic conditions. Revival provides a cultural glue that toughens the myths of Celtic unity, because revival and the critical need for revival, through archaeological intervention into the past and repackaging in the present, serve as omnipresent themes in the writing of Celtic history.

The musicians who perform Celtic music and stage its revivals have skilfully determined the ways these factors of unity can be woven into music and conveyed to audiences who wish to encounter Celticism in its most quintessential vocabularies. Texts in Celtic languages obviously provide one of the ways in which music draws upon the store of unifying factors. The crucial issue is not understanding Irish or Scottish Gaelic, or Welsh or Cornish, but

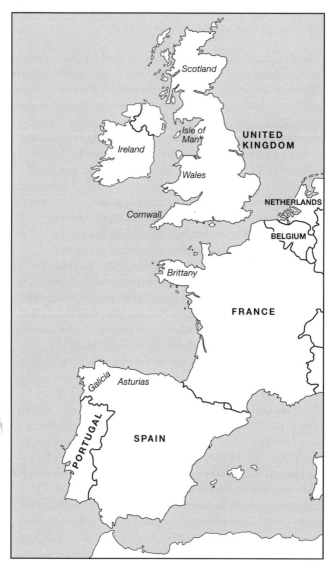

Map 1. Europe's Celtic fringe

rather finding assurance that these languages provide narrative contexts for the myths underlying Celtic music.

Musical instruments, too, provide icons of unity for Celtic music. The instrument most commonly employed to represent the ancient qualities of Celtic music is the harp, the symbol of the great bardic traditions, whose singers are believed to have wandered throughout the Celtic lands singing the epics that conveyed history through oral traditions. The instrumentarium for Celtic dance music, too, displays a high degree of unity, stretching from Scotland in the north to Galicia and Asturias in Spain, the southern extreme of Europe's Celtic fringe. In theory Celtic music should not be devoid of certain instrument types, for example bagpipes, which appear in local variants as different as Scotland's Highland pipes and Ireland's *uilleann* pipes. Attempts to integrate the musical traditions of Spanish Galicia have emphasized the survival of bagpipes in the northwestern province of Spain, strengthening their presence by encouraging Galician pipebands to organize themselves for participation in Celtic music festivals. Musicians themselves and a Celtic aesthetic of music must also be considered as factors that unify myth and history. Musicians acquire credibility as Celtic by emphasizing authenticity, on one hand, and by consciously recontextualizing authenticity through revivals, on the other.

Celtic music spreads across a geography that links Europe's Celtic fringe to the world, thereby transforming that geography into a context for world music. The geography of Celtic music-making is anchored by local sites, for example the pub or tavern in which small groups of musicians gather to perform at the core of Irish folk music, that is in a so-called 'session'. The outer limits of the geography represent the historical migrations of a diaspora, which acquires its own unity through the proliferation of the musical moments in which Celticism rallies the dispersed, for example in the innumerable festivals of Celtic music that spread across North America in the 1990s. Connecting the local to the diasporic sites of music-making are many other forms of geography, which contribute extensively to the remapping of folk music as world music. The pilgrimage to Santiago de Compostela, Spain, historically one of the oldest of all European Christian pilgrimages – Santiago marked the end of the known world when St James is thought to have reached it in the 1st century CE – has acquired Celtic meanings as one of the largest cities of Galicia. Metaphorically, this has made it possible for musicians to re-route pilgrimages to Santiago along the Celtic fringe to form postmodern confluences of Celtic religion and music (see Chapter 2).

There are no simple explanations for the remarkable transformation of Celtic music from folk music to world music. One might argue, however, that there are numerous strands of tradition – mythic and historical – that form the synapses between the folk and world music elements. Their aesthetic stances on various repertories and styles notwithstanding, practitioners and fans of Celtic music would bridle at the suggestion that it was no longer folk music. Celtic music, so its defenders argue, has never lent itself to reduction to a single sound, style, or repertory, but has always accommodated change. Forced to Europe's western fringe, Celtic peoples relied not only on their commonality, but also on their common trades as travellers along the coast who engaged in exchange of all kinds, from commercial to musical goods. Why, then, should fusion and hybridity mute the essential hallmarks of a Celtic sound? The most powerful of all such hallmarks has been inclusivity. The survival of Celtic undercurrents in North American bluegrass or country music serves as no less witness to the resilience of folk music in diaspora than to the global experiments yielding Afro-Celtic musics or 'technocelt'. Fusion and revival have historically formed a counterpoint, with alternation between authenticity and experimentation coalescing around a centre that remains unequivocally Celtic. And forming the substance of that centre, in the postmodern no less than in the premodern world, is folk music.

The Lomax family and the genealogy of American folk music scholarship

Just as there are genealogies of folk musicians, so too are there genealogies of folk music scholars. Whether one is modelled upon the other remains an open question, but there can be no question that the study of folk music accords high value to the transmission of music from one generation to the next, as well as laterally from one branch of a family to another. Genealogical metaphors fill the discourse characterizing oral tradition (e.g. the 'tune families' of Anglo-American folk song). In the course of the 20th century two families of folk musicians and folk music scholars played a particularly dominant role in the collection, publication, and dissemination of American folk music – one with Charles Seeger (see Chapter 1) at its dynastic head, the other with John Lomax playing the foundational role – and it is to the Lomaxes that we turn briefly to understand the dynamics of genealogies that sustain a broad public support of folk music during a century of rapid modernization.

John Avery Lomax (1867–1948), Alan Lomax (b. 1915), and Beth Lomax Hawes (b. 1921) all devoted their entire lives to the many branches of folk music scholarship. Although Beth Lomax Hawes was a member of the well-known folk-revival group the Almanac Singers for over a decade (1941–52), the Lomax family largely approached folk music as scholars and popularists. If there is a theoretical common denominator shared by the entire family, it was that folk music belonged to those who made it but must be shared with a broader public, thus weaving a web of culture whose strands depended on the dissemination of folk music. The Lomaxes were ideologically liberal, at times openly radical, and yet they never shied away from working with government agencies, indeed heading government agencies, willing to support folk music. John Lomax became curator of the Archive of American Folk Song at the Library of Congress in 1933, and Beth Lomax Hawes was director of the Folk Arts Program of the National Endowment for the Arts from 1977 to 1992. Above all, the Lomaxes held that folk music was a resource, and the very public nature of that resource meant that it must be shared and invested with the values of the national collective.

The publications of the Lomaxes provide a counterpoint to the history of the 20th century, beginning locally in the United States and, at the beginning of the 21st century, expanding in increasingly global directions. The history that the numerous collections of and monographs on folk music traces begins in the American West, with John Lomax's pioneering study of cowboy songs, unfolds through a series of volumes that gave voice to African Americans and the downtrodden, and shifts to broader arenas that portend globalization theory. So expansive were and are the Lomax projects that several, especially the production of CDs from the Alan Lomax 'World Library of Folk and Primitive Music', are projected to last long into the future. The influence of a century of folk music collecting and publishing is so vast that it is difficult to assess. Lomax publications from the 1930s laid the groundwork for modern interpretations of the blues, and the great 'American' anthologies served as the canon for the folk revival in the 1950s.

Whether or not folk music really narrated history, locally, nationally, or internationally, was not a matter of debate for the Lomaxes. Of course it did, if for no other reason than that one could will narrative power to accrue to folk music. The power that folk music embodied was the power of strong wills, of 'hard hitting songs for hard-hit people' or ballads and songs that could be arrogated to America's very best. For the Lomaxes, it was out of the question that folk music would lose its power or that any kind of atrophy would set in, say, if repertories fell out of fashion or if traditional singers passed on. Folk music existed to empower one to seize the moment and to make a mark on history. One could hardly ask more of folk music than did John and Alan Lomax and Beth Lomax Hawes.

The Polka Belt: a place for folk music in the world

Can world music become folk music? Turning the question that opened the above section on Celtic music on its head seems almost banal at this point in the story of this chapter, not to mention in world history at the beginning of the 21st century. Even the most optimistic and ideologically liberal collectors and performers of folk music tend to bemoan its decline and express concerns about its endangerment. With the explosion and spread of world music it might seem that folk music, yet again, is about to fall victim to the very hegemonic forces to which it has so liberally contributed.

Polka, however, tells a different story about the relation between folk and world music. The complexity of polka as a folk dance of international proportions blurs the distinctions between folk and world music and belies any attempts to classify it with convenient stylistic and cultural categories. In a word, polka is found – and it is danced – just about anywhere in the world that Western music as folk, popular, and classical music has penetrated. With polka's geographical epicentre in the northern part of today's Czech Republic, the dance spread throughout the Austro-Hungarian Empire and was passed on by emigrants, travelling musicians, and later even the salon music of European colonizers to the rest of the world. Wherever it travelled, polka musicians domesticated the dance, adapting it to local social functions, ensemble structures, and aesthetic parameters. Wherever it was played, the polka became local; after its travels around the world, it again donned trappings as folk music. Once relocated and relocalized, polka's functions as folk music proliferated. It might assume a new identity through a new name; it surely underwent processes of cultural change and engendered new variants; it influenced other styles, enriching their local character; and it would win over new listeners and, especially significant, new dancers.

There is no single explanation to account for polka's remarkable malleability and adaptability, for its insistence on reasserting folk qualities. Two general perspectives, however, prevail. We might regard the first perspective as top-down, for it calls attention to polka's inclusivity as a multiethnic, multicultural, and multigeneric music. According to this perspective, polka is not so much a style arising from a dance form – duple meter in generally ternary forms (variants of ABA) – as it is a cultural and sound aesthetic that stretches as an umbrella over musics that express collective identity. Those espousing the top-down perspective point to the prevalence of designations such as 'polka music', which draw in far more styles and repertories than polka. In contrast, there are perspectives that approach polka from the bottom up. At the centre of polka style there are certain traits that allow anyone and everyone to participate in its performance, as musician, dancer, listener, or generally as an aficionado. Polka is thus the music of the collective or the folk, and as such it expresses the collective consciousness.

Both perspectives shed light on the geographical formation known as the 'Polka Belt', a cultural region defined by polka music that stretches from the Dakotas of the USA and the prairie provinces of Canada to the ethnically diverse urban centres of the East (Map 2). The Polka Belt encompasses a geographical region of considerable girth, where cultural and ethnic diversity is the norm. Musical styles move fluidly along the Polka Belt, from notch to notch, and styles coalesce through processes of exchange and cross-fertilization. A number of factors contribute to these processes. Musical and ethnic style combine to express the unique character of polka at a given notch, for example the popular 'push style' that has developed in Chicago under the dominance of Polish Americans such as Eddie Blazonczyk or the accordion-heavy Slovenian style of Cleveland, home to Frankie Yankovic.

Polka style is also institutionalized at each notch, for example by the dance halls and social organizations that support concerts and dances. The social venues for polka may be local, ethnic clubs and churches, or even polka clubs themselves, or they may connect the local to an international scene, for example through the activities of

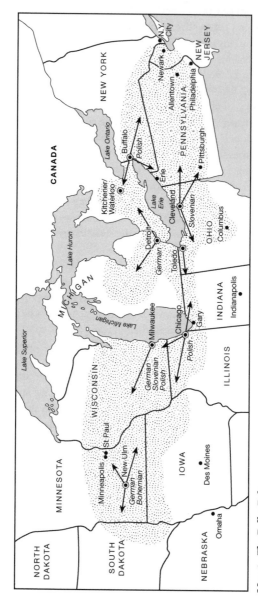

Map 2. The Polka Belt

the International Polka Association (IPA) or the events announced in the pages of magazines and newspapers such as *The Polka News*. The historical popularity of polka music – polka must be regarded, too, as a folk music that is also a popular music – depends on extensive mediation. Publishers of band parts and sheet music, radio stations, and local and national recording companies produce and reproduce polka music, disseminating it across long distances while maintaining bases of operation at the notches of the Polka Belt. The media have remained effective because of their ability to parallel the globalized mediation of popular music, for example by winning a category for polka in the annual Grammy Awards in 1986.

The Polka Belt, finally, is by no means isolated to the American Midwest and Northeast, and to ethnically diverse provinces in neighbouring Canada. Other geographical regions defined by polka have emerged on the landscapes of world music, for example the Texas-Mexico border regions, where various *conjunto* fusions have transformed polka while retaining its quintessence. The cities of the Polka Belt swell with Mexican immigrants at the turn of the 21st century, with new polka styles taking shape along the new cosmopolitan borders between ethnic and working-class groups.

World music is one of the places in which folk music functions like folk music. By examining the folk music landscapes formed of local, regional, and global components, such as the Polka Belt – or waltz-*Ländler* complexes in East Central Europe or the spread of *ghazals* across the Islamic cultures of West, Central, and South Asia – we witness the ways in which the global actually replenishes the local. Understanding the relation between folk and world music may require far more than simply disabusing ourselves of the notion that world music produces a cultural grey-out that consumes folk music. Folk music and world music clearly replenish each other; in some parts of the world they may even depend on each other. Both the survival and revival of folk music have benefited from the spread of world music, and world music in turn has proved to be far more hospitable to folk music than anyone could have predicted.

Chapter 5
Music of the nations

The Eurovision Song Contest

Whether or not a song can really represent a nation on the international stage of cultural politics seems not to concern the organizers, performers, and audiences of the annual Eurovision Song Contest. The stakes are simply too high not to accept the nationalist potential of world music. Staged each year since 1956, the Eurovision Song Contest brings together the representatives of all member nations in the European Broadcasting Union, as well as the representatives of nations who have other reasons for allying themselves with the pan-European cultural politics of popular song. From the outset Eurovision Song Contest organizers emphasized the ways in which the event would foster European unity where, in the political climate of a Europe divided along the faultlines wrought by the Cold War, there was little unity. The political idealism of the contest, nonetheless, created an aesthetic dilemma: how can a popular song evoke the spirit of the nation and yet suppress all traces of nationalism? It is this question, writ ever larger across a globalized musical landscape, that complicates the relation between world music and the modern nation-state.

The roads leading to the annual broadcast of the Eurovision Song Contest come from several directions. For the participating musicians the road starts locally and regionally, through a series of contests, which may take place on the stages of smaller festivals or at the initial stage of judging submissions from aspiring (but well-established) songwriters. A sifting and winnowing process occurs, and eventually, usually in the late winter, the winning entries in each nation compete in a nationally broadcast competition, from which the winner is chosen according to a democratic system of judging, and is charged with representing the nation. The roads of the Eurovision Song Contest itself wend their ways across Europe, with the broadcast taking place on a Saturday evening each May in a large auditorium in the host country, the previous year's winner. The roads from the national broadcast entities themselves are, perhaps, the least comprehensible on the public map of the contest, but it is they that determine the direction European unity will take at any given historical moment. At the top are the national broadcast networks, the members of the European Broadcasting Union, which coordinate the broadcasts and the voting by telephone that will determine the winners.

The performers reach the evening of the contest itself after months of hype and lobbying, during which the national entries are broadcast countless times throughout the continent, giving the eventual arbiters of world music taste, the citizens of Europe, the chance to make up their minds long in advance. Finally, the Saturday evening of the broadcast – European and Eurovision primetime – unfolds as a series of performances, each one framed by opportunities for the audience to acquaint themselves more intimately with the national representatives. Closing the evening is the voting, in which national commission after national commission calls in its nation's votes. The votes are tallied, and a new Eurovision winner is chosen.

The Eurovision Song Contest is the single largest popular-song competition on an international level. Though limited to Europe, however broadly defined, the contest has no real competitors elsewhere in the world, thus making it possible to regard it as a sort of Olympics of popular song. During its almost half-century history it has always pushed at the international boundaries of Europe, attracting Eastern European nations whenever possible (in fact, rarely so) during the Cold War, opening its stage to Mediterranean nations allying themselves with European cultural politics, and making gestures toward racial and ethnic inclusivity, for example when France submitted entries from its *départements*, or semi-autonomous colonies, in the Caribbean.

The musical and political landscape of Europe charted by the contest thus constantly changes. Just how the winners and, by extension, the public profile of national song change, however, is another issue altogether. The rules governing the structure and contents of an entry change almost year by year. For many years, an entry could not be in the national language of a country that was not deemed to be international, and accordingly most winning entries have been in either English or French, arguably a reason that Anglophone and Francophone nations have won most often (30 times during the first 45 years of the contest). Sometimes the rules are more innocuous on their surface, for example in the early years of the contest when backup singers were prohibited or discouraged; the biggest international hit not to win the contest, Domenico Modugno's 'Volare' in 1958, failed to place well because of this restriction. The shifting regulations notwithstanding, winning entries tend musically to sound rather similar. Structurally, many employ a standard verse and refrain alternation, punctuated by a 'middle eight', where the song becomes fleetingly more interesting. There is no requirement that an entry must bear a musical relation with the nation it represents in the contest; the 2001 first-prize winner, Estonia's 'Everybody' (Tanal Padar, Dave Benton, and 2XL), employed a pan-Caribbean dance-hall sound, call-and-response throughout, and a sprinkling of expletives from the American South. Texts, too, are often innocuous on their surfaces, which has in turn led to the frequent insertion of nonsense syllables (here, 'Volare', with its memorable refrain, 'Volare, wo ho ho ho, cantare, wo ho', might be familiar as a case-in-point to many readers).

So, where is the nation? Or the better question might be, what is the nation? To arrive at some tentative answers to these questions we might first consider some winners and losers. Probably the two most famous Eurovision winners that went on to international careers have been ABBA (1974) and Céline Dion (1988). ABBA's winning entry, 'Waterloo', conformed perfectly to the winning model of the mid-1970s, a rock-style song that would succeed effortlessly in the Anglophone pop charts. Céline Dion, a Canadian, performed the Swiss entry in 1988, 'Ne partez pas sans moi', which stylistically was a detour from the Celtic-flavoured repertory (and its appropriation to fictionalize the Celtic diaspora, for example in the film *Titanic*) with which in large measure she would make her career. For Dion, nonetheless, there were nationalist issues embedded in the French-language Swiss entry, which lent itself to interpretation as a symbol for the national aspirations of French Canadians in Québec.

Whose nation, we might then ask? For Israelis, who have historically been one of the most competitive participants in the Eurovision contest, the question is rather more unequivocal, if the answers have not been. Winning the Eurovision Song Contest provides Israelis with a means of asserting their Westernness on the stage of world politics. It is hardly surprising that Israelis virtually shut down the country on the evening of the contest, and that the Israeli CD market is flooded with compilations of once and future Eurovision winners. Not geographically connected to Europe, Israel is musically very connected to world beat, as witnessed in the career of its most famous international star to emerge from the contest, Ofra Haza, who narrowly came in second place in 1983 with 'Chai'. With 'Chai' Haza launched a career that took her farther and farther away from the long tradition of Yemenite-Israeli singers who had emphasized the Easternness (*mizrakhiut*) of Israeli popular music, a direction that she herself reversed in the late 1990s when she began again to reintegrate Yemenite traditions prior to her early death in 2000.

What kind of space does a Eurovision entry make for the nation? There have been a few notable cases of highly politicized national spaces, for example in 1989, the year of the Velvet Revolution, when Yugoslavia, one of the few East European competitors, entered Riva's 'Rock Me', thus giving the Eurovision voters a chance to make a public statement about the political upheaval sweeping across Eastern Europe. The nations on the stage of the Eurovision Song Contest have, with few exceptions, been primarily monocultural, not least because multiculturalism would initially have to be a statement by the competing nation about its identity. Change comes slowly to the contest, but there may be evidence of growing acceptance of multicultural nations, for example in 1999, when Germany's entry to the contest in Jerusalem was the Turkish-German singer, Sürpriz, an acknowledgement of the country's multigenerational workforce containing Turkish guest workers. Sürpriz managed to finish in second place with 'Kudüs'e seyahat' ('Journey to Jerusalem'), a song that played on the German children's game, *Reise nach Jerusalem*. In the many covers of the song, Sürpriz mixed languages (Turkish, German, Hebrew, and English) and both secular and sacred symbols, the competition for musical chairs in the German children's game, the pilgrimage to a city holy for the Jews of the host country, the Christians of the national entry, and the Muslims of the Turkey of Sürpriz's ancestors. 'Kudüs'e seyahat' bore many of the earmarks of a Eurovision entry, and yet it was a song less crafted for victory than for re-examining the very national questions upon which the Eurovision Song Contest had been predicated. It made no pretence about the reality that such questions were complicated and that world music, even when mustered to the service of a nation's international image, could not be easily dislodged from the nation or from nationalism.

The singing nation

Each, every, all, whole. The power of music to connect a people to the nation lies in the pervasiveness of adjectives. Each nation aspires to discover and gather its own music. Every citizen of the nation enjoys the cultural legacy afforded by song. All nations of the world celebrate the universality of music by bringing their national musics to the international stage. The path from individual musical identities to world music passes through the nation; the cultural and historical crossroads beyond the local yields to the global. That roadblocks form at the crossroads of the nation is also part and parcel of the geography of world music, for just as the nation admits to the power of inclusive adjectives, it bends also to the oppression of exclusive adjectives. Not every resident of a nation is afforded access to all songs. Each ethnic group may prefer its own music to that of the whole nation. Taken as a whole, all musics of a nation may provide sufficient room for each music. The nation's position at the crossroads is as often troubled as it is celebrated.

There it is at the crossroads anyway. Indeed, there may well be no more common sign and symbol for world music than the nation. The parsing of world music as national music is as old as the nation itself; or perhaps, more to the point, as old as nationalism itself. When Johann Gottfried Herder (see Chapter 2) first forged a vocabulary to describe world music, he drew upon national concepts. Herder's vocabulary was critical because it established a process of inscribing world music, transforming it from an oral phenomenon to a national language through the employment of written procedures. The processes of inscribing world music may have become more technologically elaborate at the beginning of the 21st century, but they continue to privilege the nation as what would appear to be the most stable space on the map of world music. The *Rough Guides* to world music, the most widely used compendium of global popular music styles, takes the nation as its organizational principle, with the reader touring the world recording industry by turning the pages from nation to nation (see Chapter 7). When musicological and ethnomusicological reference works at the beginning of our century – say, the 10-volume *Garland Encyclopedia of World Music* or the 29 volumes in the second edition of the *New Grove Dictionary of Music and Musicians* – expand the surveying tools for understanding world music, they may add conceptual categories, but they resolutely refuse to abandon the nation.

The nation is an ontological fact of life in the study of world music, even in an era when nationalism has increasingly become a dirty word. Nationalism can often be, of course, the not-so-soft underbelly of national music. Nationalism, positively or negatively construed, enhances the exclusivity of national music. Rather than representing the nation as a whole and serving purposes beneficial to everyone, nationalist music acquires more specific functions, perhaps the dissemination of a restrictive set of ideological values or the aggrandizement of a ruling ethnic group or an élite oligarchy. Music presents the nation with a way of preserving its past and thus writing the history of its present. We witness acts of preserving the nation in the designations by Japan and South Korea of musicians who are 'national treasures', whose performance and teaching must be supported to prevent national musical traditions from disappearing. National musics rendered as nationalist musics may lead a nation to war or attempt to claim land and history that belong to someone else. By injecting nationalist sentiments into national music collections, scholars and government agencies alike *ipso facto* make room for some residents of a nation while taking away space from others. The darker sides of nationalism, too, offer explanations for the persistent presence of the nation in world music.

It is not only the nation that shapes national music. Music, because of its performativity, can powerfully shape the nation. To explain this performative power of music Benedict Anderson has coined the term, 'unisonance', the sonic moment that occurs when people from throughout the nation gather in a shared performance of music. Crucial to Anderson's notion of unisonance is that each singer may not fully be aware of the extent to which she or he is joining with others throughout the nation. The unisonant moment may occur when a national anthem is being sung at a state ceremony. We might add to Anderson's nationalist examples the broadcast of

Eurovision entries over state broadcasting networks, which have the effect of encouraging everyone (e.g. riders in sundry forms of public transportation) to sing along. Unisonance effectively connects the adjectives that describe national musics, allowing 'each' person to sing the music of the 'whole' nation with 'all' other citizens.

The nation joins together as a singing nation. The communal experience of music-making generates a feeling of cultural intimacy, what Michael Herzfeld describes as the 'social poetics' of the nation-state. Significantly, it is not one genre or repertory of music (e.g. folk music) that lends itself to cultural intimacy, but virtually all kinds: popular, religious and classical music, vocal and instrumental music, the most revered historical repertories and newly created hit songs. When the nation joins in the performance of the musical styles it deems its own, it effectively breaks down the barriers between repertories that might have been exclusive to one segment or another. For these reasons, folk song finds its way into symphonic poems, and sacred songs become national anthems. The music of the nation stimulates cultural mobility, a closing of ranks around shared experiences.

As concepts such as unisonance and cultural intimacy make clear, national music is also fundamentally collective. It is hardly surprising that choruses often take it upon themselves to perform a music that unequivocally projects nationalism. Welsh choruses, for example, have long maintained repertories and concert practices that intentionally draw attention to Welshness. Choral singing provides a consistent public venue for using the Welsh language. By opening their ranks to blue-collar workers and intellectuals alike Welsh choruses collectively represent a cross-section of the Welsh population. The circuit of festivals and competitions that ritualize the seasons and the annual cycle, moreover, acquires distinctively Welsh qualities, which extend to diasporic Welsh communities, such as those in the United States, where Welsh choruses serve as the primary vehicle for maintaining – and performing – Welsh-American identity.

Choral movements give shape to the nation, but not merely as a matter of representing the nation. They can – and in times of high nationalist tension do – mobilize the nation to action. In the years leading to and then following the independence of the Baltic states of Estonia, Latvia, and Lithuania from the former Soviet Union, choral music played a particularly visible role in staging political action, both symbolically and physically. So powerful were the Baltic choral movements that they are frequently described as 'singing revolutions'. National history intersects with national myth to empower the choruses to crystallize the forces of revolution. Accounts of singing festivals may exaggerate, but the point they make about a revolutionary social poetics fired by unisonance cannot be missed. The description in one of the most widely distributed CDs of world music from post-Velvet Revolution Eastern Europe is typical in every sense:

The mobilization of the nation is also contingent on the mobility of the choruses. One of the most characteristic features of national choruses is that they go on tour and take part in competitions. It is hardly coincidental that nationalism spawns choral 'movements'. At competitions they join with other choruses to renew their musical resources and engage in the cultural work of the nation with like-minded choristers. The mobility of the choral movement in the New Europe also serves ethnic and national communities without nations. Turkish guest workers in Germany, for example, frequently give public performances of repertories arranged for chorus, even though choral music is not traditional in Turkey. Since the early 1990s a Jewish chorus movement has developed in Europe, usually with choruses forming around a synagogue or confederation of Jewish social organizations. Jewish choruses are notable because of their visibility and mobility, and they travel extensively, retracing the historical connections between the cosmopolitan centres of Jewish life largely decimated by the Holocaust. The Turkish choruses of the New Germany and the Jewish choruses of the New Europe are not attempts to mobilize the nation. They inspire, instead, a type of reflection on nationalism as both inclusive and exclusive, and they remind us that the choral music of peoples without nations also contributes powerfully to the shaping of the nation.

Dana International: national music without borders

> We have become two nations and, it's true, for many people I have come to represent freedom, democracy and the right to live how individuals want to live.
>
> > (Dana International, January 1998, upon being chosen to represent Israel in the Eurovision Song Contest)

On 9 May 1998, the Israeli entry won first place in the Eurovision Song Contest, broadcast that year from Birmingham, England. 'Diva' was sung by Dana International, an Israeli whose mixture of Yemenite and Sephardic heritages had located her in a lineage of popular singers familiar to Israelis, beginning with Beracha Zephira in the 1930s and 1940s, and most recently sustained by Ofra Haza, who, like Dana, had represented Israel well in the Eurovision Song Contest, though, unlike Dana, had not been victorious in 1983. Times had changed, however, and Dana International had a national image rather different from the earlier Israeli stars popularizing *musica mizrakhit* (eastern music).

On the one hand, Dana was demonstrably patriotic, and she openly displayed her eagerness not just to represent Israel but to win for Israel. On the other hand, Dana was famously transsexual, and she was no less open in her display of a complex sexuality. In a religious state, whose orthodox and ultra-orthodox religious population commanded an extraordinary degree of national power, one might expect that the image of a nation embodying multiple forms of sexuality would not be particularly welcome, especially on the stage of the most widely broadcast world music contest. Born a male but living her life as a female, famous in the Muslim countries of the Middle East as Sa'ida Sultan for both Arabic and Hebrew lyrics, known for the gay undertones of her earlier torch-song days in Tel Aviv clubs and the multisexual overtones of her more recent techno recordings, Dana International stood fast by the nation in the international arena. And by the time of the Eurovision Song Contest, she had succeeded in winning over the nation.

The nation, both universally as a cultural entity and locally as a political state in the Middle East, assumes many identities in Dana International's music. If there is a stylistic and textual theme that unifies Dana's songs, it is the nation – the nation in its multiple forms. It is that nation, for example, that the 'Diva' of 1998 Eurovision winner embraces. The 'Diva' of the title has many identities 'because she is larger than life', and she has been present in the lives of many famous women – Maria, Victoria, Aphrodite. In her signature tune 'Dana International', which appears in two versions on the 1993 CD of the same name, Dana International fashions her identity as a world traveller, who journeys from Saudi Arabia to Monaco, Paris, and Mexico, all on the way to Tel Aviv, the end of her journey. The song affirms the nation where many identities are possible, and she strengthens her claims by alternating the techno beat with instrumental interludes that use a *takht* ensemble to map traditional Arab music (*mūsīqā al-'arabiyyah*) on the nation. Dana's songs mix and remix the nation, sampling the elements that have always constituted the multiple histories of Israel's past and the multiple identities of its present. In so doing, they confirm rather than deny a national presence in Dana's own vision of world music. It was that vision that her victory at the 1998 Eurovision Song Contest so clearly recognized.

National anthems

NAVY DEPARTMENT,

Washington, October 18, 1889.

SPECIAL ORDER:

John Philip Sousa, Bandmaster of the Band of the United States
Marine Corps, is hereby directed to compile for the use of the
Department the National and Patriotic airs of all Nations.

B. F. TRACY, Secretary of the Navy.

(Cited as an epigraph in Sousa, 1890: xi)

At one of the deepest levels of our popular-culture subconscious we
all share a common image of national anthems: the victory
ceremonies at the quadriennial Olympic Games. There, on
platforms in full view of the international media, stand the victors,
struggling at once to hold back tears and to mouth the words of
their national anthems. It's a moment of national pride framed by
music. The moments are often memorable; the national anthems
are often less so. For observers aware of the international musical
scripts of the nations of the world, the most memorable musical
aspect of the Olympic victory ceremonies may be the occasional
instances when the wrong anthem is played.

Is anyone really listening, and does anyone really care? To answer
these questions I turn in this section to one of the most widely
distributed of all types of world music, the national anthem. In the
history of nation-building, there have been many who have, in fact,
cared a great deal about national anthems. Many anthems have
enjoyed long histories; many nations have inscribed their histories
in amazingly complex ways by selecting and discarding, revising
and recomposing, their national anthems at multiple moments of
national crisis. In the aftermath of the attacks on the World Trade

Center in New York City and the Pentagon on 11 September 2001, the American national anthem, 'The Star Spangled Banner', came to open virtually every public event, not only commemorative ceremonies and the usual athletic events, but also concerts of most orchestras, even when on foreign tour. National anthems are serious business, and it is for that reason that they are performed at the most solemn moments dedicated to performing a nation's essence.

When we hear national anthems, not to mention when we really listen to them, we are nonetheless struck by a paradox: Don't they all sound rather alike? At public moments of patriotic pride, when the identity of the nation really is at issue, one might expect some striking differences. Even more striking, the most recently created (or chosen) national anthems for the post-colonial nations of Africa and Asia do not sound ostensibly different from the anthems that have been around for several centuries. To confuse the matter even more, there are the anthems of different nations that are, in fact, the same, as well as those that have consciously borrowed melodic motifs and phrases from other anthems. It would seem almost as if there were a subconscious awareness that national anthems, at some level, *should* sound alike.

If, for example, one traces the histories of national anthems, it is clear that many came to exist when rupture and crisis were motivations for their creation. When Rhodesia proclaimed independence from Great Britain in 1965, it naturally discarded 'God Save the Queen' and detoured briefly through the international territory of the Beethoven/Schiller 'Ode to Joy', before Zimbabwe, well over a decade after its independence, adopted 'Yumi i glat blong talem se' in 1994. There are both textual and contextual reasons that national anthems may sound rather alike. First of all, many new anthems are based on previously existing anthems, even when these are meant to serve as an intermediate stage in the creation of a new anthem. The most common models have been England's 'God Save the Queen', France's 'La marseillaise' and Franz Joseph Haydn's 'Kaiserhymne' (the Austro-Hungarian Empire's anthem until World War I, and Germany's since 1922). International anthems (see the final section of this chapter), too, have served as models for national anthems, notably the 'Internationale' and final movement of Beethoven's Ninth Symphony. Second, though the anthems are of distinct genres (e.g. hymns, marches, or fanfares), performance practice tends to create a high degree of homogeneity, for example by scoring national anthems for wind ensembles playing in a stately style. Third, anthems may sound alike because they are played at occasions more alike than different, for example at state ceremonies or athletic events, in the theatre or cinema, or to punctuate national and international radio and television broadcasts. Finally, there is the aesthetic issue that Malcolm Boyd states rather baldly, namely that both texts and melodies are universally rather uninteresting.

The history of national anthems parallels that of nationalism, unfolding through a series of historiographic stages, beginning with the Enlightenment in the 18th century, Romantic nationalism (especially in Europe and Latin America) in the 19th century, colonial expansion from the late 19th century until World War II, and post-colonialism from the mid-20th century to the present. At each of these stages the national anthem meant something different, and it was crafted to signify nations in different ways. Typically – an adverb I use because of its relation to the most common adjective applied to national songs, 'typical' – the earliest national anthems captured some of the sound and function of folk songs. In the middle stages, national songs aspired to religious and military genres. During the post-colonial stage, national anthems characteristically attempted to embody a modern nation's history, both the *longue durée* and the recent struggle.

National anthems appeared in two different ways, which together are suggestive of the multiple meanings that converge when a nation is given voice through song. The first of these ways would seem on its surface to be most familiar to us: a nation decides to proclaim its nationhood through song, and it sets a composer, or, not uncommonly, a lyricist to the task. Whereas we might imagine that the national anthem does not easily win widespread approval, we do not necessarily assume that the final product results from contentious debates, from experiments that are more often than not rejected, and from a final compromise that amounts to the least of several evils. Part of the problem results from the fact that the collectives attempting to carve out a national song may be more ideologically than musically inclined; the suggestions of the more musically inclined, moreover, may be rejected out of hand for their lack of ideological correctness.

The other way in which national songs come into existence might be compared to the use of a massive vacuum cleaner that is shoved in the direction of everything imagined to fulfil some characteristic of the national. We notice this approach because it often begins by producing anthologies or repertories the sum total of which collectively represents the nation. In such anthologies, 'our' national melodies often mingle with 'theirs', locking self and other in a process of mutual style demarcation. In 1854 on the occasion of her wedding to Emperor Franz Joseph, for example, Empress Elisabeth of the Austro-Hungarian Empire received a volume of beautifully engraved songs that was a compilation of the empire's 'national melodies', which together portrayed the complex linguistic and cultural regions of Eastern Europe. The staging of international events, for example world fairs or cultural congresses, commonly generated anthologies of national songs. The epigraph that opens this section similarly set in motion a collecting project that would lead to a publication of national songs from throughout the world in a volume presented by US Marine Corps Bandmaster John Philip Sousa to the US Navy Department and, by extension, to the American people. We might marvel at such a project, and expect that its fulfilment as a 'Special Order' from the Secretary of the Navy would lead to a very superficial potpourri of melodies, but in fact the 283-page volume is executed with meticulous detail and carefully crafted harmonizations and arrangements, all accompanied by copious footnotes and ethnographic information. The final six pages, for example, contain national songs from Wales, Wallachia, Yap Island, Zamboanga Island, and Zanzibar, sources that might not easily find their way into modern ethnomusicology anthologies, historical or otherwise.

There is nothing simple about national anthems, and to illustrate precisely this point let me briefly sketch the very equivocal path along which one of the most unequivocally charged of all modern national anthems, known as the 'Deutschlandlied', or 'Germany-Song', but called by German- and non-German-speakers alike, 'Deutschland, Deutschland über alles' ('Germany, Germany, above all else'), developed. We have already made our acquaintance with the 'Deutschlandlied' in this section, for its melody, called the 'Kaiserhymne', first served as the source for the anthem of the Austro-Hungarian Empire. The 'Emperor's Hymn' was composed as a movement of a string quartet in 1797 by Franz Joseph Haydn, who had for many years served as court composer for the Hungarian Esterhazy family, whose summer residence was in Eisenstadt, a largely Jewish city in a Croatian part of West Hungary. The melody, at any rate, derives from a Croatian folk song, variants of which today survive in the Croatian parts of Burgenland, the Austrian province in which Eisenstadt is the capital. We could linger a bit while discussing the 'Kaiserhymne' in the Austro-Hungarian Empire, but instead I shall jump ahead to 1841, when August Heinrich Hoffmann von Fallersleben, a school teacher from Silesia (today in southwestern Poland), wrote the poem, 'Deutschland, Deutschland über alles', while in political exile on the island of Helgoland in the North Sea, at that time held by England. We're tempted to ask, then, what was German about the song destined to become the German national anthem? Paradoxically, it might well be that the nationalist reception of the song played a role secondary to its international origins. Whether or not it is world music according to narrow definitions is not the question, but rather how its journeys, as one of the most identifiable and oft-copied national anthems, entered those chapters in the history of world music articulated clearly and contentiously by national anthems.

The IFMC/ICTM: to each nation its music

The International Council for Traditional Music (ICTM) has historically regarded its name with no less ambiguity than its 'official' object of study: 'to assist in the study, practice, documentation, preservation and dissemination of traditional music, including folk, popular, classical and urban and dance, of all countries'. Calling itself the International Folk Music Council (IFMC) at the time of its founding in 1947, the IFMC renamed itself as the ICTM in 1981, opening the generic boundaries of its subject matter and dismantling the boundaries of what many members regarded as Eurocentric disciplinary practices. However sweeping these moves toward conceptual reorganization were, they left the political organization of the most wantonly international society devoted to the study of world music intact. The broadly defined musical object – stretching from folk to classical to urban – necessarily found itself in 'all countries'. At the core of the ICTM's cultural politics has been the nation, which takes the institutional form of 'national committees'. ICTM international politics, too, take place at the borders between nations, above all through affiliation with organizations such as the International Music Council and UNESCO. However an individual member chooses to study world music, the ICTM locates it in the nation, or rather 'all countries'.

The scholars (and musicians and dancers) who have contributed to the ICTM, whether as dues-paying members, participants in conferences, or 'study groups', or as elected or appointed members in the ICTM polity, do so as representatives of their nations and world music in their nations. In the early years of the IFMC, world music in the nation was broadly subsumed under the rubric, 'folk music', a designation that the publications of the organization reproduced. Early issues of the *Journal of the International Folk Music Council* (later the *Yearbook of the IFMC* and then after 1981 the *Yearbook for Traditional Music*) included article upon article that located folk music in the nation, clearly attempting to cover as many nations as possible during the post-World War II era. Cooperative ventures, such as collaboration with UNESCO in producing a series of world music recordings, with LPs for all regions and nations of the world, shored up national boundaries with other genres and practices of music, initially classical musics (e.g. in Asia) and in the closing decades of the 20th century hybrid and popular musics (e.g. in Latin America). By the turn of the century, the vocabulary of globalization theory increasingly suffused the geographical categories in ICTM publications, but to question rather than dismantle the nation (e.g. in the 1999 *Yearbook for Traditional Music*, for which globalization is loosely a special theme).

The nation-derived historiography of the ICTM is not, however, nationalist, and in this sense it bears witness to the paradox we have been tracing through this chapter. 'Folk music' and 'traditional music', like 'world music', aim to embody some quality of music that is international, in other words that crosses national borders, but as ontological categories of music they are simply too general and too generic. In attempting to cross national boundaries, even when these are called international boundaries, they call attention to those boundaries, indeed, to the political problems that coalesce around them. The ICTM wrestled with those problems by actively finding the financial means to bring members from countries with communist governments, especially in Eastern Europe, to conferences. The discursive border-crossing of the ICTM broadened its conceptual categories, increasing the presence of world music in a scholarly society initially devoted to folk music and dance by mapping it against a grid of nations, the music of each one equal to that of its global neighbours.

Beyond the nation – super-, supra-, and international anthems

> It is the final struggle, join together, and tomorrow.
> The International will be Mankind.
>
> ('l'Internationale', original chorus, 1871)

For aesthetic, ontological, and political reasons national music rests uneasily at the borders of the nation. National music complicates the relation between the nation and world music, giving way to the super- and supranational conditions of nationalism, and to the creation of genres that, for the purposes of this book, we might call 'international anthems'. International anthems exist in a complex counterpoint with national songs. There are times when they bolster each other, in moments such as the Olympic Games, when the 'Olympic Anthem' (composed by Spiro Samara in 1896) represents a global community of nations, while the national anthems represent the constituent members of the community. Some international anthems serve as voices in the contrapuntal history of national anthems, at times surfacing as a surrogate national song – frequently the case of the 'International' in the Soviet Union – alternately arrogated to national causes and politicized as international causes. National and international anthems are not the same, but one depends on the other, and only together do they fully connect the nation to world music.

Songs usually do not become international anthems overnight. International anthems may not be born as such, but the myths that are spun by those who adopt them generally portray them as destined to become such. Breaking down the musical and textual traits of international anthems does not necessarily explain which traits do or do not prove most effective as stylistic building blocks. Melodies may or may not contain characteristics that reflect an international character. When compared to national anthems, there might be even fewer cases that depart from common-practice uses of tonal harmony. On one hand, some of the most widely used international anthems have rather complex melodic structures that make them rather difficult to sing; this is true of the 'International', which requires a rather wide melodic range of the singer, who might also find it rather difficult to navigate complex rhythms and wide intervals. On the other hand, international anthems are, with very few exceptions, choral works. Though they require concerted performance by a mass of individuals whose cultural and musical differences may be extreme, they do not therefore make it particularly easy to perform the world through song. Maybe that's the point.

Specific historical moments usually engender the chain of events that shape and reshape an international song. An anthem itself may or may not directly participate in those moments. In the case of the 'International' the song and the events are virtually inseparable. The text of the 'International' issued from the pen of Eugène Pottier, who wrote the poem during the French suppression of the Paris Commune in 1871, when one of the first great communist experiments was crushed. The melody and original setting of the song were the work of Pierre Degeyter, a textile worker and choral director from Lille, who, legend has it, unearthed a collection of Pottier's 'revolutionary songs'. For the worldwide socialist movement, which quickly adopted Degeyter's setting of Pottier's poem as an anthem, the pedigrees of worker and musician were extremely important, in effect meaning that the song could mobilize the very struggle from which it was born.

The history of the 'International' was indeed international from the outset. Labour unions adopted it, as did socialist organizations of all kinds. It symbolized the struggle of the voiceless, and it quickly gave them voice by undergoing countless translations and settings. The 'International' was very much a song about encounter, between tradition and modernity, and in an era of expanding colonialism between the West and those occupying the farthest corners of its empires. When socialist workers' movements turned into communist political movements and when these inspired revolution, the 'International' was there, on the frontline of political action. For a socialist vision that sought to unify the world, the 'International' musically implemented that vision, in Europe, South America, Africa, and Asia.

The world united by the 'International' was a loose ideological and political confederacy, and part of the anthem's efficacy might well have been its ability not to bind that confederacy too tightly. There have also been international songs whose lives began on the level of loose confederacy, but have followed an increasingly narrow path toward nationalism. This was surely the case with the song 'Ha-Tikva' ('Hope'), which channelled several musical and textual streams on its way from song of the international Zionist movement to Israeli national anthem. Already at the first Zionist Congresses in the late 19th century, 'Ha-Tikva' had found its way to the cultural stage of an international Jewish organization that was still relatively inchoate. The song changed all that, for by encouraging the delegates to join together in song – as a body of choristers from throughout the world – the early Zionists created a common voice. That the song's own birth was shrouded in circumstances that would prevent the movement from realizing it was a synthetic pastiche, forged as a single song in 1886 by Naphtali Herz Imber, was more musically than ideologically relevant. The song's ambiguous melodic and tonal structure allows it to signify numerous histories, from folk song to national song to easternness (hence, the common association with Bedřich Smetana's *Moldau*). When 'Ha-Tikva' became a national anthem for Israel, that too was a natural result of its symbolic power, which allowed it to shift from international to national in a process that paralleled the in-gathering of immigrants from throughout the world.

Forging international anthems has become a preoccupation of many attempting to create policies of regional and global unification at the turn of our own century. As with previous attempts to map the nation onto the world while obscuring the nation's borders, the synthesis of postmodern international songs requires a fusion of myth and history, as well as the fictional reworking of both. There is perhaps no more immediate example of the attempts to forge a song to celebrate the international than the tales that spin about the creation of an anthem to represent the unification of Europe. It was the composition – actually the completion – of a *Concerto for the Unification of Europe*, for example, that provided the central narrative for Krzysztof Kieslowski's film, *Bleu*, for which Zbigniew Preisner composed a score that turns the anthem inside-out, then reconstructs it so that the grand European chorus at the end can sing forth its biblical text (Corinthians I, chapt. 12, verses 1–13). Here, however, we are departing from facts entirely.

The tales about European anthems also include a few facts. The European Union does not have an official cultural policy, but rather an official hands-off policy, stated as Article 128 of the 'Treaty on European Union' thus: 'The Community shall contribute to the flowering of the cultures of the Member States, while respecting their national and regional diversity and at the same time bringing the common cultural heritage to the fore'. It is also a fact that many international musical activities happen under the unofficial auspices of the EU. Whether the use of the Beethoven/Schiller 'Ode to Joy' is one of those lies at the border between fact and fiction, where myth and history intersect. It is a fact that a sort of mystical consensus exists about tapping Beethoven's setting in his Ninth Symphony of Schiller's Enlightenment paean to universal brotherhood. There had previously been suggestions about using the 'Ode to Joy' as an anthem of the UN. Already in 1972, Herbert von Karajan had undertaken an arrangement of the 'Ode to Joy' for the Committee of Ministers of the Council of Europe, but at that time it found little consensus, not least because of Karajan's very public history as a former participant in Nazi cultural activities. Again, facts have assumed mythical proportions. Stylistic questions also arose, for example about the real nature of Beethoven's international style in the final movement of the Ninth Symphony, which is notable also for its orientalist style, not least the insertion of a Turkish march; would this represent the Turkey desiring EU membership or the Turkish guest workers of Central Europe?

The question remains, then, Whose nations and whose world might international anthems unify? Will the political ends of national music be inclusive or exclusive? In the case of the European Union will it be necessary to reconsider the inclusivity of its anthem when new members from Eastern Europe join its ranks? The Beethoven/Schiller 'Ode to Joy' does not answer those questions, but it certainly poses them. National music and nationalism in music have historically been extremely public phenomena, for they seize the stage of history, perhaps in choral movements that mobilize political movements, perhaps in battles between colonizer and colonized about the legacies that narrate the present and future. The stakes for claiming the stage of the nation with music are very high indeed.

Chapter 6
Diaspora

Diasporic re-encounters, 1492–1992

1492 was a year that proved to unleash diaspora upon diaspora. It was in 1492, of course, that Columbus 'discovered' the New World, which soon thereafter became a colonial space virtually defined by its alterity, the fact that it was not the Old World. With the New World opened for colonization, new possibilities for settlement were set in motion, some advantageous for the Old World – establishing new trade networks or escaping religious persecution – most disadvantageous for just about everyone from other 'worlds' that did not enjoy the historical privileges quickly gained by Europe in the Age of Discovery. Many of the same conditions that stimulated Columbus, other explorers, and the aristocracies that financed global discovery proved particularly disadvantageous for the Others who had occupied European soil for centuries. In 1492, the *reconquista* – the retaking of the Iberian Peninsula from the non-Europeans and non-Christians who had lived there for centuries – also came to a dramatic conclusion when all Muslims and Jews were forcibly driven from Spain and Portugal. In the century after 1492 human displacement was massive and worldwide, and it established diaspora as one of the defining conditions of early modernism.

During the centuries of the early modern and the modern eras, the

'92s', those years that mark the passing of another century since Spain's historic unleashing of diaspora, have generated considerable celebration, which has been accompanied by considerably less reflection on the displacement we have come to call diaspora. The 92s witness world fairs, for example, which assemble cultures from throughout the world and put them on display. The cultural endeavours of the years leading up to a celebration in the 92s are necessarily global in proportion, if for no other reason than the almost banal fact that 1492 was the first consciously historical moment of world history. The music mustered to mark and celebrate a 92 celebration is, by extension, world music. At the 1893 World's Columbian Exposition in Chicago (so massive was the fair that organizers needed an extra year) there were countless performances of world music, and at least 103 of these appeared on the first systematic recordings of world music at the fair. In 1892 (or 1893) there was little discussion of diaspora per se, but much recognition of the world dominance that the West had maintained since the conquest that followed 1492.

In 1992 the celebrations were again vocal and global. The New World threw itself a birthday party, and in the Old World Spain, especially, missed few opportunities to announce the global role it had played 500 years earlier. At the 1992 anniversary, however, questions of displacement and diaspora were addressed more critically. The modern era of colonialism had largely come to an end, even as nations of the Third World – a formulation that critiqued previous distinctions between 'New' and 'Old' – struggled with the post-colonial heritages inherited from the 'First' and 'Second' worlds. It was in 1992 that more open judgment on the expulsion of Jews was passed. The designation of the expelled Jews, *Sephardic*, found a new currency, even though few realized that the Hebrew *Sephard* is no more nor less than 'Spain'. In the historical reassessment of Sephardic culture, nonetheless, there was full recognition that the traces of that culture spread across a landscape of diaspora roughly equivalent to the Mediterranean and its littorals. Sephardic Jews had clung to the shores of the

Mediterranean, moving when necessary, and it was often necessary.

Sephardic culture was diasporic, indeed, all the more so because it formed from a previous diaspora, necessitated by the destruction of the Temple in Jerusalem in 70 CE. In the historiography of the Jewish diaspora, the Sephardic diaspora within a diaspora had remained relatively unknown in comparison with the history of Ashkenazic Jews in Central and Eastern Europe, and with the history of the modern nation-state of Israel. All that changed in 1992 was that Sephardic history took its place as one of the ways of re-encountering 1492. This act of revisionist historiography happened almost overnight as Sephardic music was elevated to the status of world music. Sephardic music lent itself to rediscovery precisely because it was the music of diaspora. It had survived because it was portable. Sephardic folk music, especially, was narrative, with genres such as the *romance* and *romancero* weaving historical accounts into the stories of ballads. 1992 was a moment of revival, with singers – Sephardic or not, Jewish or not – seizing upon the collections of Sephardic song and recording them as traces of the diasporic past, for example as 'vistas of the Balkan', whose Sephardic communities at the time were rapidly disappearing because of the civil war sweeping through the nations of the former Yugoslavia. For Sephardic music, 1992 marked the moment of transition to world music.

The Sephardic diaspora was by no means the first to possess the potential dimensions of a world music. The term 'diaspora' itself had a long currency, originally referring to the dispersion of classical Greek civilization from the central city-states to the peripheral islands and colonies. Jewish history, too, was interpreted from Jewish and non-Jewish perspectives as diasporic. 1992, nonetheless, marked a watershed, and the rediscovery of Sephardic music was just one of the most visible traces of that watershed. Almost without anyone's noticing it, many different cultures and human displacements had acquired the characteristics – and name – of a diaspora. There were, for example, African, Irish, and South Asian diasporas. Important for our considerations in this book, the musics of such diasporas began to display the characteristics of diaspora. They were mobile, and their histories inscribed the boundaries and routes of migration that formed the landscape of diaspora. The musical traits of diaspora laid claim to a position in the world, and that position became a requisite context for world music. Diaspora became a musical context for encounter, migration, and fusion.

The diasporas of the 1990s reflected the historicism of 1992 and previous 92s in different but distinctive ways. In the present chapter three diasporas will serve as leitmotifs, each historicizing different moments of the encounter formed by modernity and globalization. Not least because it has been addressed so powerfully through re-encounter, the Sephardic diaspora, the direct consequence of the expulsion of Jews from Europe, serves as the first leitmotif. The African diaspora formed along a different set of historical faultlines that spread from the conquest of the New World, for the displacement of Africans resulted from the use of slaves to fuel the economic engines of colonialism. Already during early modern globalization, it had become almost impossible to stem the impact of African music on the earliest forms of world music. The South Asian diaspora draws upon music to represent the historical implosion of the post-colonial world. Its processes of displacement and its sites of encounter are in some ways highly localized, especially in the cultures once dominated by the British Empire, but the music of the South Asian diaspora increasingly contributes to and draws from world music.

It almost seems as if diaspora, as a political, historical, and musical condition of modernity, was unchecked in the 1990s. To deny a culture, displaced or not, the status of a diaspora on some level was to deny it a place in a global culture. It is hardly surprising, then, that diaspora itself became a context for world music, and that it has come to play a role in shaping world music. In the 21st century diaspora itself offers a place where world music takes place, nurturing and emphasizing its very placelessness.

Diaspora, place, and placelessness in world music

Diaspora is a condition of placelessness, and as such it has become one of the places most articulated by world music. The music of diaspora at once describes the conditions of being displaced from a homeland, and it inscribes the history and geography that connect a displaced culture to that homeland, or at the very least to a place claimed as home. The music of diaspora is about places of being and places of becoming, of connecting the present with its absence of place to the past and the future, where place can be imagined as real. The process of imagining a sense of place to supplant the condition of placelessness necessarily produces hybridity and fusion formed from juxtaposing repertories gathered along the path defining diaspora.

Diaspora assumes very diverse forms, but it is possible to describe three very general forces that bring about the need to leave a place regarded as a people's own. First, there are religious reasons leading to the expulsion from a place of origin. The journey from that place of origin assumes sacred dimensions, above all because providence requires that the journey eventually return to the place of origin. Some of the historically oldest diasporas, notably the Jewish diaspora, have become profoundly sacred precisely because of the promise of return. Second, there are peoples and cultures with no place to call their own, thus making it necessary to move ceaselessly. Again, there are classic cases of such diasporas, those of Roma and Sinti peoples being very well known. Third, there are more modern diasporas spawned by socioeconomic reasons. The widespread emigrations and immigrations following from the breakup of empires and the conflicts of nationalism are among the chief causes for the third type of diaspora.

Drawing upon W. E. B. Du Bois's notion of African American

double consciousness, Paul Gilroy has suggestively theorized the 'Black Atlantic' as a conceptual space in which cultural traits with both African and non-African origins interact to produce diasporic histories and geographies. Double, or perhaps even multiple consciousnesses, make it possible for groups to maintain cultural practices that express connectedness to an historical homeland while responding at the same time to new homelands. The musics of Du Bois's Afro-America or Gilroy's 'Black Atlantic,' thus can differ radically from each other, yet share certain common traits, which in turn become the stuff of a common history. Double consciousness is anything but historically schizophrenic, for a crucial element of consciousness remains anchored in shared traditions derived from notions of what is crucial to the diasporic experience. Music, as Gilroy and other theorists of multiple consciousness have been quick to demonstrate, emerges as one of the most powerfully symbolic forms of common tradition. If music survives as a trace of the homeland, it also provides a means of negotiating with outside cultures in the diasporic environment. In short, music maps itself on both consciousnesses and becomes a way of explicitly expressing diaspora.

Musical instruments often serve as some of the most palpable traces of origin in the diaspora. In the African diaspora musical instruments accompanied slaves freighted across the Middle Passage, and the memory of instrumental practices and ensembles were revived across the Americas as slaves and former slaves employed music to remember the past they shared with their ancestors. Xylophone-type instruments, with wooden and metal slabs, have long served as evidence for the retention of instruments from West African ensembles. Xylophone-type instruments, furthermore, have provided empirical evidence for connecting African concepts of rhythm and time to African American and Afro-Caribbean musics. In East and Southeast Asia, other instruments and instrumental ensembles have played important roles in the inscription of diaspora. Chinese silk-and-bamboo orchestras have followed the maritime routes of Chinese trade and settlement in

Southeast Asia. The metallophone orchestras of Southeast Asia (e.g. the Javanese gamelan) also reflect diasporic patterns, for they have spread throughout the region, where they express linguistic, economic and musical connections.

The diasporic patterns of musical instruments are not simply a matter of dispersion and dissemination. Exchange across the borders between multiple consciousnesses is often even more significant. The instrumentarium of the South Asian diaspora provides one of the most complex examples of exchange and the concomitant web of connections between homeland and diaspora. Musical instruments have historically played a significant role in the crossing of religious, linguistic, and social borders in South Asia, bearing witness to the complex historical consciousness of South Asian culture. With the colonial era, entirely new and seemingly foreign instruments were imported to India. If many of them quickly found their way into Indian musical practices, it was not, by and large, because they were imposed. The violin and clarinet found their ways into Karnatak (South Indian) classical music, while the harmonium established itself in the light classical and devotional music of Hindusthani (North Indian) music. Widespread export of musical instruments followed on the heels of the diaspora produced by the post-colonial era. Accordingly, sitars (long-necked plucked lutes) and tablas (a set of two small drums) from Hindusthani music found their way quickly into Western jazz and rock 'n' roll (we need but remember George Harrison in *Norwegian Wood*) and South Asian genres of worldbeat. The harmonium, its Western origins notwithstanding, now charts the South Asian diaspora, so much so that the world centre for harmonium manufacture is Kolkata (formerly Calcutta).

Throughout this chapter, and indeed this book, we witness the ways in which the explosion in world music is paralleled by the proliferation of diaspora. When we ask why this is, we find ourselves greeted by quite complex answers, many of them rather disturbing. First, there are more groups who consciously give unity to otherwise barely related patterns of immigration by remapping them as diasporas. Ethnic Irish abroad, for example, have increasingly begun to refer to themselves as an Irish diaspora. Some of the new diasporas may well be inventions, for example the Celtic diaspora, but they nonetheless bespeak a deep concern about the recognition of double and multiple consciousness. Clearly they also bespeak the fragmentation that has produced an alarming spread of placelessness in an age of competing nationalisms. World music offers a musical place for the narratives of diaspora, be they national or religious, or the results of violations of human rights. Just as there are 'new diasporas' in the 'New Europe', for example, the musics of those diasporas are most audible and effective as world music. This has surely proved to be the case with the Muslim diaspora in Central Europe, the South Asian diaspora in the UK, and the North African diaspora in Spain and France. For many stateless peoples, for example the Kurds, whose homeland straddles the borders of Turkey, Syria, and Iran, world music has temporarily transformed the placelessness of diaspora into a place for expressing common history. In an age when diaspora has itself undergone globalization, world music has incorporated structures reflecting multiple consciousness, so much so that world music is increasingly about placelessness and return.

Bob Marley: weaving the diasporic web

Diaspora unfolded like concentric rings during the course of Bob Marley's career. Marley (1945–1981), at the centre of diasporic rings, consciously wove together the stylistic mix of musical styles that intersected in the Caribbean. The synthesis that Marley achieved was the spinning of a diasporic web, which drew its strands from musical, historical, ideological, and religious sources, connecting Jamaica and the Caribbean to Africa and Europe, confronting the encounters of colonizer and colonized, slave master and slave. Marley's mixtures of ska and reggae, his impact on rock and rap alike, his evocations of Rastafarianism and resistance, might well have collapsed under the weight of their own eclecticism had he not discovered a common theme to bind them together, diaspora.

Bob Marley's life itself unfolded with the dimensions of a sacred journey. The stations of his short life were many, each one allowing him to draw upon the complex histories that intersected in his personal life and in the public arena of Jamaican music. The son of a black mother from rural Jamaica and a mixed-blood father from the urban administrative class, in his youth Bob Marley absorbed a particularly Jamaican form of double consciousness. His formative years were spent in rural Jamaica, but in his early teens he moved to Kingston. By the age of eighteen, he had formed the core of his band the Wailers. Already before the production of his first ska album in 1965, he had released several hit songs, the best known of which are 'Simmer Down' and 'Put It Down'. The broad outlines of Marley's life are relatively well known. Instrumentalists entered and exited from the Wailers, but the configuration known as Bob Marley and the Wailers remained more or less intact from the late 1970s, when they made a series of groundbreaking albums: *Rastaman Vibration* (1976), *Survival* (1979), *Zimbabwe* (1979), and *Uprising* (1980). After a long struggle with cancer Marley died in 1981, since which time his visibility as an icon of diasporic musics in the Caribbean has proved unassailable.

Bob Marley came to symbolize the double consciousness of diaspora by making several different kinds of connections to Africa, but the primary quality of each was to underscore the commonality of Jamaicans and Africans. Both were engaged in struggle, at one level against the forces of historical oppression, slavery, and colonialism, and at another against global economic politics. Marley also turned to the religious domain of diaspora, notably in his intense involvement with Rastafarianism, the symbols of which came to form the metaphorical path of a return to the Africa of the earliest black Christians. The musical path for that return moved from metaphorical to real in the stylistic changes heralded by Bob

Marley's music, from the reworking of African *akete* drums in the rhythm of ska in the early 1960s to the integrative Africanness of rock steady in the late 1960s to the full articulation of a Jamaicanized Rastafarianism in reggae by the early 1970s. By reworking the symbolic presence of Rastafarianism, Marley recharted the journey of Jamaican popular music, mapping reggae as a music of diaspora.

Music's place in the South Asian diaspora

But when a Rajasthani sings [Rag] Maand, or a Punjabi sings [Rag] Sindhi Bhairavi, he returns to his homeland, which for him is a certain landscape influenced by seasons, a certain style of dressing and speaking, a web of interrelationships and festive occasions.

(Amit Chaudhuri, from *Afternoon Raag*, 1993: 217)

The epigraph opening this section comes from a novel about diaspora, Amit Chaudhuri's *Afternoon Raag*, the story of a Bengali student at Oxford, whose own relationships with English education and with the many other Indians studying and living in England unfold as a brilliantly mirrored series of vignettes. The narrative thread that binds the vignettes, the snapshots that together constitute a *Bildungsroman*, is music. Interspersed among the encounters with friends and lovers are the accounts of music lessons at the home of the narrator's teacher, a brother of his *guru* in India. The narratives of *ragā* – the Hindusthani system of melodic modes signalled in the novel's title – are laden with journeys that enable the narrator to draw closer to India at each lesson and through each rehearsal of the rāgs appropriate to the afternoon hours when the lessons take place. The rāgs upon which the narrator reflects bear witness to both the diaspora, with its sense of placelessness, and to the places in India itself, specified by each distinctive rag, 'a self-created galaxy of notes'. For the narrator the rāg is doubly referential, at once conveying the unsettled character of journey and anchoring the material essence of Hindusthani and Bengali music to homeland. To experience the rāg in the afternoon lessons is also to return home. The afternoon rāg, in Oxford so modern in its traditionality, embodies both home and diaspora.

Properly speaking, the dispersion of South Asians has produced not one, but many diasporas. The diasporas bear witness to a multitude of origins: indentured servitude in the 19th century, particularly responsible for the growth of Indian populations in the Caribbean and in the British colonies of eastern and southern Africa; the political implosion of the subcontinent in the mid-20th century; the emigration of Pakistanis and Bengalis in search of economic opportunities elsewhere; and the brain drain of South Asian intellectuals and scientists to the West, which began in the 1970s and shows few signs of abating. Culturally speaking, the South Asian diaspora is very mature. It has a literature of its own, with authors such as V. S. Naipaul and Salman Rushdie already serving as avuncular figures for a younger generation, often born and educated in the diaspora itself. The maturity of the self-reflection these writers weave into their fiction and criticism alike has exerted a profound effect on South Asia, where the language of the diaspora, English, has, arguably, become the primary language of the literary homeland.

Musically speaking, South Asian music also has a mature presence in the diaspora. Many Indian and Pakistani musicians spend as much time abroad as at home, not just performing but also teaching. For children born in the diaspora, especially in the urban and academic centres that serve as nodes in the diaspora's web, it is not particularly difficult to learn traditional Indian music or to study the classical-dance form, *bharata nāṭyam*. The LPs of an older generation of South Asian musicians, of Ravi Shankar and Ali Akhbar Khan, are familiar throughout the West, but so too are the CDs of a younger generation that has lived almost entirely in the West, for example Sheila Chandra and Zakir Hussein. The 'musical maturity' of the South Asian diaspora is possible because music has mapped it on so many different places that together make up the diaspora. Music, Amit Chaudhuri's 'self-created galaxy of notes' and more, also connects those places, paving the way for journeys within the diaspora. It is to a brief description of some of those places that we now turn.

Point of origin and return

At first glance, it may seem paradoxical that musics of the South Asian diaspora identify their places of origin as specifically as possible, rather than simply referring generally to India, Pakistan, Bangladesh, or Sri Lanka. Bhangra (see below), no matter how extensively it has fused with other world musics, is traced to Punjab. Establishing a point of origin makes a crucial statement about authenticity. By specifying the point of origin, moreover, the possibility of return becomes more tangible. South Asian points of origin also connect the several diasporas that run parallel to the modern South Asian diaspora, not least among them the historical and musical journey of Rom people, which, as in the film *Latcho Drom*, itself framed as an historical journey charted by music, began in Rajasthan.

Myth and religious narrative

The sacred and secular stories of South Asian music propel it along the path of diaspora. The stories of the *Rāmāyaṇa* and the *Mahabhārāta* epic cycles open narrative spaces for the journeys of Hindu mythology's constellation of sacred actors, and music, explicitly in song texts and formal structures, absorbs the stories. In the diaspora myth and religious narrative find their way to new settings, for example Hindu temples in North American suburbs, where new generations learn *bhajan*s, or in Sufi shrines of North England and Scotland, where new and old saints are praised by resident and travelling troupes performing *qawwali*.

Classical music societies

The institutional structures of colonial India frequently provided models for the organization of Indian classical music, first in India and then beyond in the diaspora. At the beginning of the 21st century there are organizations supporting South Asian classical music throughout the diaspora. Supported by voluntary membership but not infrequently through government arts funding, the classical music societies have local functions, organizing the teaching and performance of music in a city or small region, and international functions, providing concert opportunities for musicians on tour. Musically, the classical music societies have become products of the diaspora, for more often than not they depend on – and facilitate – the consolidation of musical practices across regional and religious boundaries in India and Pakistan. Concerts billed as 'South Meets North' have become standard features of diaspora music societies, be they in the UK, Singapore, or Cape Town.

Indian cinema

The Indian cinema is the most globalized site for the production and consumption of South Asian music. Often described with a variety of statistics as the largest film industry in the world, 'Bollywood' relies extensively on film music, which developed from musical theatre and has extended to film musicals in all the major languages of India. The incorporation of music into Indian film is nothing if not eclectic, and, accordingly, it has become one of the primary forms of musical entertainment in the diaspora. Indian films and film music appear regularly on several international media networks. In more localized centres of diaspora, nonetheless, video cassettes, sold and rented in grocery stores and newsstands, bring the music of Indian cinema into each home and family.

Media and mediation

The sale of video cassettes of Indian cinema is just one way of transforming music into a language of mediation between homeland and diaspora. The subcontinent enjoyed one of the earliest recording industries in the world, relying on the international potential of early transnational companies (e.g. His Master's Voice and EMI), but also developing local and regional distribution networks. The spread of the South Asian diaspora in the 20th century was paralleled by the extension of recording and other media networks, thus making South Asian music readily available wherever South Asian communities were found.

Popular music, fusion, and border crossing

Considered as a whole, the places of music in the South Asian diaspora form a landscape that encourages rather than stems change. Music defines place not by isolating it, but rather by opening its borders so that different genres, styles, and repertories, some South Asian but others not, cross the borders and cross-fertilize one another. It is diasporic border crossing, for example, that produces *chutney* and *bhangra*, which I discuss in the final section of the chapter. The place of music enriches the conditions for the processes of change that come to narrate the history of diaspora itself. These processes, in turn, most frequently lead toward popular music.

A. Z. Idelsohn and his musical monument of Jewish diaspora

Gathering the music of diaspora in a single anthology and publishing it as a representative monument of diaspora would seem like an improbable, surely futile, undertaking. This was, nonetheless, precisely the task which Abraham Zvi Idelsohn (1882–1938) set himself in 1907, when he first arrived in Jerusalem with a wax-cylinder recording machine from the Academy of Sciences of the Austro-Hungarian Empire. Over the course of the next few years, Idelsohn would work and teach in Jerusalem to support the research that had brought him to Jerusalem: systematic recording of music sung and played in Jewish communities from throughout the diaspora – from Morocco in the west to Bukhara and Daghestan in the east – who had settled in the *yishuv* (or 'settlement') in the eastern Mediterranean. The task confronting Idelsohn was to document, one way or another, the various theories about the ways in which music could represent the diaspora itself. At one extreme, there were those who held that music preserved the past, not least because of the ability of Jewish communities in diaspora to sustain the quintessence of their past by living in relative isolation. At the other extreme, there was a need to gather empirical evidence that might account for the differences between Jewish musical practices in those areas of the diaspora that were relatively well known, especially Ashkenazic and Sephardic traditions.

The diaspora project occupied Idelsohn for the next quarter century of his life. In one way or another, it shaped his research and publication, and his teaching in Europe, the United States, and South Africa. The destabilizing circumstances of the First World War, the rise of fascism and anti-Semitism, and several immigrations of his own did not deter Idelsohn from publishing his musical monument to the Jewish diaspora, the ten-volume *Thesaurus of Hebrew-Oriental Melodies*. Volume by volume, the *Thesaurus* moves systematically across the diaspora. The first five volumes encompassed the traditions of Jews from Yemen (vol. 1), Central Asia (vol. 3), and North Africa (vol. 5), among others. With the second five volumes, Idelsohn returned to traditions that were closer to his own heritage as a Latvian-born cantor who had built a career in Germany, where he also studied musicology: here were volumes devoted to the 18th-century German synagogue (vol. 6), the folk songs of Eastern European Jews (vol. 9), and the songs of hassidic Jews (vol. 10). The *Thesaurus* was monumental at every level. Idelsohn transcribed and published his wax-cylinder recordings, and he extracted melodies from texts in manuscripts handed down by Jewish cantors of many generations. He established historical connections and plotted them on systematic analytical tables. He applied theoretical models from historical musicology and comparative musicology, and from these he speculated about scalar structures and the cultural practices that either did or did not reveal that the diaspora was unified by music. Idelsohn raised more questions than he answered, however, questions that have proved crucial to the recognition of Jewish music as a world music undergirded by diaspora and, by extension, established diaspora as foundational to Jewish-music scholarship ever since.

Select glossary of world musics shaped by diaspora

arabesk: dominant style of Turkish popular music, formed at the intersection of folk and classical traditions, and at the intersection of various ethnic, regional, and international traditions. Arabesk represents various patterns of mobility within Turkey, from east to west, from rural to urban, and it serves as an emblem of Turkishness for Turkish diaspora communities, especially 'guest workers' in Europe.

bhangra: historicized folk dance from Punjab (northwest India), which is presumed to retain a symbolic gestural vocabulary of agricultural practices. Globally, bhangra is a set of popular styles in the South Asian diaspora that consciously invite fusion, for example in exchanges with reggae and Jamaican dance hall.

chutney: hybrid Caribbean popular music, especially in Trinidad, which combines styles from the South Asian and African diasporas. Chutney permits many different sounds and repertories while mapping South Asian instruments on public events and festivals with significance for Afro-Caribbean culture.

dangdut: Indonesian popular song, drawing its ethical content from Islam, the dominant religion of Indonesia, but its musical style from Hindi film songs. As a modern genre, dangdut thus bears witness to the intersection of several diasporas in Indonesia.

ghazal: a poetic genre, usually employing couplets, that has spread across the Islamic world, from the Muslim Balkans and Turkey in the west to South Asia and Southeast Asia in the East. Ghazals rely on classical imagery, but texts are most often in vernacular, albeit literary, languages, thus permitting extensive crossing between stylistic borders.

hip hop: general term used to describe African American popular musics that critique the oppressive conditions for blacks in American cities. Hip hop developed along a stylistic path that accommodated fusion, mediated by the alteration of LPs and recorded sources by DJs and rappers. Also widely known as rap.

klezmer: Jewish popular music, historically associated with the rituals and dances of weddings in the Yiddish-speaking communities of Eastern Europe and North America. Klezmer has entered a diaspora of its own that historicizes the world of European Jewry destroyed by the Holocaust.

mestizaje: general term describing the presence of Chicano (Mexican American) elements in the Hispanic American popular musics. Mestizaje undergirds the complex patterns of hybridity Tex-Mex, *conjunto*, 'crossover' etc. – that have propelled Hispanic musics into the popular-music mainstream of North America.

musica mizrakhit: the popular music of 'eastern' (*mizrakh* = East) Jewish communities in Israel, both of North Africa and of the Middle Eastern Arab nations. The eastern sound forms around the deliberate incorporation of instruments, musical structures, and texts that emphasize easternness, thus a form of cultural resistance to the hegemony of western, Ashkenazic Jewish culture in Israel.

raï: popular music of urban North Africa, above all from Algerian and Moroccan entrepôts, which has formed a musical canon for the North African Arab diaspora (see Chapter 3).

reggae: Jamaican dance music, shaped from the mediation of local dance styles, such as *ska*, through the mixing boards

> of dance hall disc jockeys. The distinctive Jamaican sound of
> reggae provides a template for various diasporic musics in
> the Caribbean.
>
> *zouk*: dominant popular dance style of the Francophone
> Caribbean. Zouk musicians have used local recording studios
> and radio stations to mix popular styles from throughout
> the Caribbean, which in turn have followed musicians to
> the diasporic communities in France and returned to the
> Caribbean with even more extensive hybridity.

During mid-summer 2001 Asian Diasporas enjoyed a disturbing
presence in newspaper headlines throughout the world. In the
American Midwest, on one hand, the Asian diaspora was able, for
the first time, to claim a fair share of the cultural stage with the
sundry other ethnic communities that had employed world music
to set the process of 'festivalization' in motion, one of the primary
symptoms of the transformation of immigrant and ethnic culture in
the USA to diaspora culture. The 'First Annual Asian American
Cultural Festival' inserted itself into the summer festival season of
Chicago, sponsored by the Radio Voice of Asia and the several
diasporic communities whose music and dance ensembles would
perform throughout the final weekend of July. The Asian American
fare ranged from 'camel rides' and 'native fashion shows' to
Bangladeshi and Pakistani folk dance to the 'Philippines Dance
Troupe' and 'Indian Snake Dance'. The festival took place in the
Devon Avenue neighbourhood, historically the crossroads of
numerous diasporas: now heavily South Asian, Devon is
historically Eastern European Jewish, and most recently it has
attracted Korean, Hispanic, and Middle Eastern communities. The
emphasis of this festival (as opposed to the emphasis on '*bhangra*
aerobics' in the 'Punjabi Sports Festival' two weeks later) was on the
uses of music and dance to perform diaspora. The performing
organizations were distinctive because of their lack of

distinctiveness. What they shared lay at the root of their performances, and what they shared was diaspora.

Diaspora in the UK occupied international headlines during the summer of 2001 in quite a different way. Historical tensions between 'Asians' and 'youths' grew to the breaking point, giving way to 'nights of unrest' and 'riots'. The inverted commas provided ways of ameliorating a more disturbing set of cultural circumstances, namely that the 'Asians' were residents of northern English cities, where they lived in communities shaped by one of the oldest and most extensive South Asian diasporas. At times, the word 'race' was also inserted into the inverted commas, and as such it served also as an emblem of diaspora, the historical concern, by no means limited to the UK, that diaspora is also about race and the fear of racial others, as well as about the economic disadvantage that placelessness too often produces.

The festivals and performances, and the riots and Balkan border conflicts (e.g. between Macedonia and Albania), equally served to move race and diaspora to a common stage during the summer of 2001. Race and diaspora often – too often – intersect, above all because both are about competing claims for place and about the consequences of placelessness. Indeed, race and racism have dominated the histories of the three diasporas with which I used to connect the different parts of the present chapter, the Jewish, African, and South Asian diasporas. Throughout the chapter we have observed that diaspora has increasingly become a cultural and political condition in the post-colonial world, and that it has become one of the most global contexts for world music. We should like to feel that these are all grounds for celebrating diaspora and world music all the more. Celebration, however, will not erase the racial components of diaspora, nor will it mask the unceasing racism that greets diaspora. The world musics that emerge from diaspora should and do force us to confront these profoundly important questions, reminding us that the experience of world music has very serious implications for the places opened for peoples in diaspora.

Chapter 7
Colonial musics, post-colonial worlds, and the globalization of world music

Street musicians in the new Eastern Europe

Early each weekday and Saturday morning, merchants gather in the marketplace of Cluj Napoca, Romania, to sell their wares. Surrounded by the sterile and crumbling cement edifices that make it difficult for Romanians to forget the socialist economy that dominated their nation from the end of World War II until the 1990s, the merchants of the Cluj marketplace sell everything, old and new, locally produced and internationally manufactured. There is a patina of pastness and folkloric authenticity that pervades the marketplace. In many booths sumptuous leather and fur goods are for sale, and cloth goods piled high and hanging on lines stretched from one booth to the next catch the eye because of the colourful needlework that leads one to believe that they are produced by craftspeople from the Carpathian Mountains that dominate central Transylvania, where Cluj is the capital city. The merchants, too, would be described by guidebooks as 'colourful' and 'folklike'. Obviously, many have arrived for the day from the surrounding villages, only to leave the city later in the day, when the market closes. If we take the guidebooks literally, 'colourful' and 'folklike' might refer to the ethnic and racial differences that abound in the market. At least four languages dominate the discussions about the sale of goods: Romanian, Hungarian, 'Ruthenian' (the Slavic language of the central Carpathians, which mixes Ukrainian and

Slovak in numerous dialects), and Romany (the Indo-European language of the Roma). There's no *lingua franca* in this marketplace, not even German and English, both of which are also heard.

Music is everywhere in the Cluj marketplace, very much a participant in the culture of commerce. Loudspeakers blare, and the merchants allow their radios to contribute to the electronic counterpoint. Some merchants have cassettes and CDs for sale, and more than a few offer handcrafted instruments, usually flutes made from wood or clay, but also more elaborate stringed instruments. Musicians ply the aisles, wending their ways through labyrinthine booths. They also use the marketplace as a staging point for forays into the centre of Cluj, dominated by a cathedral square and the once-proud Baroque architecture of a university city. The music of the street enters the everyday world of Cluj from its market. The musicians know only too well just where they can set up their portable stages in order to attract the most generous audiences. They know which repertories will best sell to Cluj's many students, and they are sensitive to not making a false step by drawing attention to the longstanding frictions between Romanian- and Hungarian-speaking residents. The street musicians are even more aware of the new audiences in the city, the growing numbers of tourists who are visiting Transylvania and Romania since the fall of the Ceaușescu government in 1990. Eastern Europe entered a period of dizzying transition in the 1990s, and Romania's street musicians were quick to make the most of it.

The street music of Cluj Napoca is world music in the most modern sense. It is global music performed locally. Its juxtapositions and unpredictable mixtures are postmodern. If one looks and listens long enough, one will encounter musical evidence gathered from every part of the world. The street musicians are good at marketing themselves; they are professionals, and their stock in trade is a capacity to adapt themselves to the changing currents of a multicultural society. The street music of Cluj is also traditional in any sense we might choose to use that term. Many musicians playing on the city's streets in the day return to villages at night or on the weekends, when they play for dances, weddings, or other rituals that constitute traditional folk culture. Whereas many musicians rely on recent technologies, say for producing cassettes and CDs of their own, they also play instruments made by local instrument builders. Where else would they find handiwork and tuning prowess to rival that of the local bagpipe builder?

The crucial point is not that these street musicians are *both* world musicians *and* traditional folk musicians, but rather that they have collapsed the difference between the two. They have not been forced into an economic situation where they choose between the local and the global, but rather, as musicians, they are able to find ways of accommodating both. For these musicians the local marketplace and the global market are at some level the same. The complex roles of Cluj's street musicians should not surprise us. Cluj Napoca's modernity and postmodernity are the products of its past, that is, of its cultural accommodation to the Austro-Hungarian Empire, to the contested cultures of Hungarians and Romanians, and to a plethora of minority groups, among whom Jews, Roma and Germans played an extraordinarily important role in shaping the city's history. So culturally complex was the past that the city has three names even today: Cluj Napoca (Romanian), Koloszvar (Hungarian), and Klausenburg (German). The traditional music has been and continues to be that of a cosmopolitan city, distinctive in its own ways, yet constantly in transition. Historically, its everyday culture projected the same cosmopolitanism that determines what world music is today, in a postmodern, global era.

At the beginning of the 21st century the encounter with world music has become an everyday experience, dominating the soundscape of the new century, 'our century'. I might even go so far as to suggest that the 'we' who are sharing the beginning of the new century are connected in no small measure because of the encounter with world music we share. There is, however, a paradox that lurks in the forms of encounter that generate globalization. If indeed we share world music globally through our encounter with it, we nonetheless experience it in very different worlds, which in turn are shaped in distinctively different ways because of economic, ethnic and racial, political and historical disparities. There are today more different technologies that enable us to encounter more world music than ever before, but the question arises as to whether these facilitate or complicate encounter. More to the point, pronouncements by media experts about the ubiquity of CDs, Internet, and the transnational recording industry notwithstanding, not everyone in the world has equal access to the technologies of world music, and most people in the world have no access. The worlds of world music, therefore, have proliferated because we can encounter them so much more immediately. To whom, we increasingly find ourselves asking, do the everyday worlds of world music really belong?

The global city and world music history

The city is the entrepôt for the encounters with world music in a postmodern world. Throughout history the city has occupied a distinctive position on the musical landscape because of the diversity it could attract and the power that put that diversity to work toward common political goals. The musics of the city undergirded its position as the centre of the musical landscape. The musical life of the premodern city might be said to possess the traits of a pre-world music. In a city dominated by trade, say, on the Mediterranean coast or along the Silk Road, the merchants who passed through were undoubtedly accompanied by musicians, and musical goods – performers and the material culture of music, such as instruments – may have constituted much that was offered for sale. As the premodern city gave way to the modern city, it developed from a musical marketplace for world music to a site for more extensive production and consumption. As print culture affected the production of folk and popular musics, particularly during the Age of Discovery and the centuries of European colonial expansion from the 16th to the late 18th century, new forms of specialization came to exert a profound effect on the diversity that nourished a city's musical life. It was in the 19th and 20th centuries, however, that urban culture underwent an explosion of truly worldwide proportions. Cities multiplied in number and grew in size. They were no longer only a phenomenon of an overcrowded Europe, but in the colonies and at the points of European expansion they began to replicate European urban structures. As the disintegration of colonial empires began in the early 20th century and accelerated later in the century, the international metropolis – what we now call 'global cities' or, more parochially, 'world-class cities' – survived as the sites of continued encounter, dominating the map of world music.

There is no single type of encounter in the global city, and it should surprise no one that the types of world music we encounter are virtually unlimited. The modern city gave the individual a greater degree of freedom to move about in the public spaces of the metropolis, and one of the most common forms of encounter is between the individual and the public spaces through which she or he has the freedom to move. The German philosopher Walter Benjamin (1892–1940) theorized the individual's encounters with the culture of the city by employing the metaphor of the shopping arcade, which in the Paris, Frankfurt, and Berlin of the early 20th century had acquired a special significance. The individual walking through the shopping streets of the city comes to know its culture by gazing at the display windows and hearing the fragments of conversation exchanged between passers-by. Music, too, is a part of the encounters made possible by the shopping arcade, for its arteries pass in front of cafés with music, theatres, and street musicians. At first glance, such individual encounters might seem random, but Benjamin suggests that they are placed in patterns by the city itself and contribute to the ways the city reflects its own time and place.

The physical topography of the metropolis also enhances the

possibilities for encounter, and no one recognizes this more skilfully today than street musicians. The world of the street musician is extremely fluid, yet bound to the street itself, as well as the other arteries along which the city's residents and visitors move. Street musicians depend on movement. Their audiences are not stationary, but rather in transit, and the music of the street must respond to the listeners-in-motion. Regulations of various kinds make it possible to stay in one spot for only short periods, but this does not necessarily work to the disadvantage of the musicians, for they have the opportunity to play for new audiences, in other words, for those who have not already given money or purchased audio cassettes and CDs. The music of the street, which increasingly enters the subways, bus stations, and pedestrian malls, only rarely belongs to the street. It is not the music of an ethnic neighbourhood, but instead is more often imported into the city. Street musicians benefit from the potential to move from city to city, and it is not

8. Street musician in a marketplace in Bucharest, Romania (1998)

uncommon for ensembles (e.g. Andean musicians in Europe) to develop vast networks that connect urban centres as if they were nodes on a global culture of street music.

The postmodern city belies the claims for global 'grey-out', because musical diversity today is, if anything, greater than ever before. It is clear that the old models of immigrant culture, with the traces of the 'old country' disappearing after three generations, were overly simplified. The city offers many opportunities for acculturation and the formation of musical hybrids. It also offers many more opportunities for celebrating diversity. Musicians in the postmodern city do not just perform in public or private settings, nor do they function within single ethnic communities or class structures, but rather they form complex affiliations that cut across socioeconomic, religious and ethnic boundaries.

The music cultures of cities today demonstrate patterns of ethnic, racial, and religious diversity that differ from one another, but grow from the distinctive ways that each city accommodates emigration from the outside, migration within the city, and the constant remixing of old and new neighbourhoods. The metaphor of 'island sounds' might effectively represent the Hispanic and Caribbean musics of New York City, whereas in Chicago continuing exchange between the city and Mexico bears witness to the special meaning of sacred pilgrimage to Guadalupe, home to the shrine to an appearance of the Virgin Mary in the late 16th century. The different colonial histories of London and Paris, similarly, have transformed them into vastly different sites for world music, all the more as post-colonialism gives way to postmodernism and still other processes of global cultural transition.

My reference at the beginning of this section to the city as an 'entrepôt' for world music was not simply a rhetorical gesture. In its original sense an entrepôt was a warehouse that served as a point for gathering goods that would be made available for sale. The encounters with world music in the city, too, are connected in complex ways to the marketing of world music. In the premodern city music acquired its diversity quite literally in the marketplace. The shops that lined Benjamin's arcades, too, were places of business. Street musicians determine where and when they perform in large part because of the financial benefits at each node along their urban musical routes. The economies of world music production and consumption will also inform the discussions in the remaining sections of this chapter, for musical tourism and the festivalization of world music are, at base, economically motivated. And if they were not, they would not have spread across the global musical landscape of the 21st century, defining ever more sharply the dominant presence of cities on that landscape.

Manu Dibango: autobiography of world music

> I have felt pushed toward others as I made my own path. It's been easier for me to fill the gap this way, I who was neither foreigner nor completely integrated into my world of origin. I was a broken bridge between two worlds.
>
> (Dibango, 1994: 2)

Born in Cameroon in 1933, Manu Dibango has enjoyed a musical career that is inseparable from the post-colonial history of West Africa and its intersection with world musics of the African diaspora. Whereas his West African roots are celebrated by France and by transnational recording conglomerates, he has perhaps always been as much a Western as an African musician. Dibango's career in world music might well be the extraordinary case of post-colonial encounter were it not for the fact that, as he attests in his autobiography, much of it was the product of a musician's life that was in several significant ways quite ordinary.

Manu Dibango spent most of his childhood in the port city of Douala, Cameroon, where his father was a civil servant, which afforded him many advantages from the French colonial government. As a child, Manu Dibango was able to attend missionary schools, and at the age of 15 he was able to go with the support of a French scholarship to further his studies in France. Whereas his early experiences were with other children in Douala, these enter his autobiography vaguely, woven into images of a past evident only as occasional traces, albeit necessary traces for the images of a world musician that accompany Dibango today. Encounter with Western music, on the other hand, accompanies the very first memories. By attending church, he writes, 'I discovered the importance of ritual and song'. His mother directed the women's choir at the church, and it was the men's choirmaster who 'gave me the magical musical virus'. So ordinary was the encounter that Dibango barely sensed its presence and impact. 'The [church] melodies were not mine, but over time I appropriated them – so much so that when I later heard Bach's *Canticle*, which I'd learned in church, I was sure it was music from home, a song from my country'.

The course of Manu Dibango's career has paralleled the post-colonial history of Francophone Africa. Soon after taking up studies in France in 1948, he supplanted the music of the colonial communities of Cameroon with new encounters, this time with African American musicians, both jazz and blues, and with French popular music and Mediterranean *chanson*. He began to study music more formally, and by his late teens he devoted more and more time to learning alto sax, which would quickly make his trajectory toward the music of black Americans unstoppable. It might be tempting to suggest that such a trajectory would destroy what few traces of African music had survived the transplantation to France, but in fact the pull toward jazz and the blues opened new opportunities for encountering Africans making music, in other words, the colonial presence of Africans in the popular music scene of post-World War II France. Dibango developed a web of musical contacts from Francophone Africa and black American expatriates in France and Belgium. His musical community included not only – and not primarily – Cameroon, but also Zaïre and other French and Belgian colonies. He would establish his playing career internationally with African American musicians – Harry Belafonte, Art Blakey, Don Cherry, Herbie Hancock – but also with white musicians, among them Paul Simon and Johnny Clegg.

Cameroon by no means disappeared from Dibango's musical activities, especially during periods when he needed to depend on the more stable income that came from playing for invitations to Cameroon. His career, nonetheless, followed an increasingly international path, undergirded by French and international record companies. His breakthrough into world music would happen in 1974, when his hit 'Soul Makossa' was nominated for a Grammy; from that point on, successes and awards piled up at an ever-increasing pace.

At the end of the 20th century, Manu Dibango became the champion of multiculturalism in world music. France and the post-colonial world in which he grew up were, more than ever, templates for what world music could become. Music itself had acquired the potential to quicken the pace of an eventual rapprochement between the West and its colonies. Dibango writes in his autobiography that

> Paris is becoming mixed-race . . . . The vibraphone goes to school with the balafon and enriches it. The tam-tam reinforces the drum-kit. Born of these sudden inventions, the musical misunderstandings between the continent and Paris finally dissipate.
>
> (ibid.: 129)

The dawn that followed the post-colonial era heralded a new age, where no music from the world need be sacrificed. 'African music was and remains a music of encounters; in this lies its attractive power'.

Recording and the technologies of globalization

Imagine for a moment what an ethnomusicologist's gallery of fieldwork would contain. On one wall there would be photographs of the people the ethnomusicologist had studied. On another there might be artifacts brought back from the field, surely musical instruments and more than likely other kinds of ritual artifacts. Then there would probably be an area in front of the third wall with display cases in which the 'music itself' was gathered, the transcriptions, tapes, and videos, amplified with evidence from fieldworkers who had previously documented the same area. Finally, there would be an area devoted to the technologies that made the fieldwork possible, with display cases full of recording machines and cameras, and with a wall devoted to photographs of the ethnomusicologist in the act of recording those with whom he or she had consulted, in other words, 'the informants'.

An imaginary museum of ethnomusicological research? Hardly. A retrospective exhibit on fieldwork in an age of colonialism? Indeed that, but more as well. Ethnomusicologists have always displayed a penchant for showing the tools of their trade and documentation of the technologies that allowed them to turn the field into a laboratory (see Figures 2.1 and 2.2). If you visit the ethnology division of a national sound archive or academy of sciences, you are likely to find several areas devoted to the fieldworker and the technologies of the field. University ethnomusicology departments, too, put their recording devices on display, at the very least those no longer adequate for the latest fieldwork. The photographs of ethnomusicologists recording singers and musicians, and collecting interviews and performances could fill volumes devoted to the field's history. Frances Densmore is seated in front of the American Bureau of Ethnology in 1916, recording Mountain Chief of the Blackfoot people (see Figure 2.1). Béla Bartók stands in a village in Slovakia, where villagers sing into the horn of his wax-cylinder recorder (see Figure 4.1). Carl Stumpf and Georg Schünemann sit with prisoners from throughout the world in a German prisoner-of-war camp during World War I, recording their songs for a global taxonomy of music (see Figure 7.3). Dominating the photographs of the ethnomusicologist at work is not so much its human aspect as the machine itself, given pride of place in the photograph in order to document something crucial about the ethnomusicologist's way of encountering the world. The recording machine is there to make a statement about authenticity, power, and the potential of the individual scholar to enter the field as an ethnomusicologist.

If we wanted to write a history of ethnomusicology by tracing the response of the field to specific technological advances, it would not be in the least difficult. As a discipline, modern ethnomusicology has come to depend on what Walter Benjamin called the 'age of mechanical reproduction'. Indeed, in the spirit of technology itself, a history of ethnomusicological technologies might provide us with an historiographic strategy that could claim all the trappings of being scientific. Technology mediates the encounter with world music, and with each technological advance ethnomusicologists gain a sense that they can gather more details about world music through encounter. It's a seductive belief, which no ethnomusicologist reasonably resists. Arguably, the field of ethnomusicology has gained in prestige because advancing technologies have allowed the field to claim a more rigorous scientific basis. There are subdisciplines within ethnomusicology, in fact, that rely almost entirely on technologies to mediate music as data for objective interpretation. Systematic musicologists trace their intellectual genealogy to 19th- and 20th-century scholars such as Alexander Ellis, who devised a system for dividing musical scales into equal measurements of frequencies, or 'cents', and Carl Stumpf, the German psychologist who established the first laboratory devoted to analysing recordings of world music at the University of Berlin.

By no means is the systematic impulse in ethnomusicology only dedicated to the scientific description of sound. Establishing the

9. Carl Stumpf and Georg Schünemann making field recordings of Tatar musicians in a prisoner-of-war camp during World War I

parameters of authenticity is equally a motivation. Can the analysis of the sound itself reveal more about what we hear and interpret as music? Can the physics of music, the representation of music as wave-form and timbral displays, transform our understanding of the metaphysics of music? Recording technology allows us – even requires us – to think in different ways about what authenticity might be. Changing technologies, it follows, produce a history of ethnomusicological ideas that reveals authenticity in constant flux.

The question arises as to whether discussions about the ethics of recording and technology can keep up with the blinding pace of technological advance. The digital technologies that flooded the global music market during the 1990s made it possible for almost anyone to enter the field to encounter world music. World music appeared everywhere on CDs and the Internet, and the sheer welter of recordings overwhelmed the legal encumbrances that might have given the listener pause for considering the ethical dimensions of encountering a world music with no other cultural context than the Internet. By raising these ethical dilemmas I do not mean to take a reactionary stance. As ethical dilemmas, which are already spawning debate and action, they are different only in kind from the dilemmas about power, appropriation, and cultural conflict that have always accompanied encounters with world music. If they arise from the technological sectors of the ethnomusicological endeavour, they are no less trenchant in the ways they require the ethnomusicologist to accept the moral responsibility of scholarship today.

The *Rough Guides* and the ethnomusicological encounter today

As if there were lingering doubts that world music had come of age with the 21st century, the *Rough Guides to World Music* rebut them from the start. In no uncertain terms the *Rough Guides* celebrate their own comprehensiveness: world music is boundless and boundaryless, and it is 'fitting that [the] new edition . . . coincides with the start of a new millennium, for it deals with the oldest and newest music in the world'. If their claims ring a bit heraldic, the *Rough Guides* nonetheless document the postmodern encounter with world music so extensively that few ethnomusicologists, from amateur to academic, from aficionado to activist, would not reasonably want to be without them. The *Rough Guides* are as much advertisement – for musicians who tour the world and their recording companies, not to mention for the travel industry that sponsors the brand of world-hopping tourism characteristic of the *Rough Guides* – as it is a real guide to the diversity of musical phenomena that it claims as its subject. Ultimately, the *Rough Guides* concern themselves far more with facilitating encounter with world music than with world music itself. Through its pages and the surfeit of CDs and websites they introduce, the ethnomusicologist of the *Rough Guides'* 'new millennium' enters the world of virtual encounter.

It would be easy enough to project a tone of pessimism and resignation about the state of ethnomusicology's approaches to world music in this final section devoted to the field and its scholars. My use of the term 'virtual encounter' might seem suggestive of technologies out of control and of music reduced to mediation alone. Anyone who turns to the *Rough Guides* will quickly find reasons to draw attention to their lacunae. Even within academic ethnomusicology, most of us love to hate the way the *Rough Guides* reduce world music and discourse about world music to so many quick-and-dirty blurbs, but few of us would deny that those blurbs rather often come in handy. All of us recognize that several of our most respected colleagues are now contributing their expertise to the *Rough Guides*, even when we have to close our eyes to the crass journalism that too often fills in the gaps. The *Rough Guides to World Music* may produce imperfect scholarship, but it is still emblematic of the ways in which the ethnomusicological encounter does take place today.

It is possible to open the *Rough Guides* just about anywhere to witness the conditions of ethnomusicological encounter today. The two volumes are first and foremost a guide to recordings and the musicians whose success has resulted from the dissemination and consumption of recordings. The issue with which ethnomusicologists today must reckon is not whether recordings wrench music from its contexts: this is what all recordings do. The recording does, however, establish new contexts, and these are attracting an increasing level of scrutiny from ethnomusicologists. As nationalism spreads in many parts of the world, recordings have emerged as an important context for supporting and resisting it. Globally, recordings and their exchange are perhaps the most vital discourse for encountering diaspora.

The *Rough Guides* also serve as a guide, perhaps unintentionally, to recent directions in ethnomusicology. Most obvious of all, they are guides primarily to popular music, and there can be little question that no area – I should go so far as to call it a subdiscipline, with its own fully articulated theory and methods – of ethnomusicology grew as rapidly and became as influential in the 1990s as popular-music studies. Growing in large part from the *Rough Guides'* privileging of popular music is a discourse that embraces and analyses hybridity, fusion, and border-crossing, in other words the conditions of globalization that are inescapable today. The *Rough Guides* could be confused for a purist's bible by no one, but, here too there is a message, perhaps a bitter one to the purist clinging to an older gospel, about the encounters that generate world music today. Finally, there can be no question that the sites of encounter are themselves vastly different. World music intensifies in immigrant and exile communities; it lends itself to ideological manipulation across the spectrum of political power; it affixes itself to revival no less than to the avant garde; it is the stuff of festival culture and tourism. The global culture that world music articulates is impenetrably dense, so much so that encounter with world music has, today, become inseparable from our everyday worlds.

World music festivals: all the world's a stage

The ethnographic present: 22 September 2001. World music as I encounter it in my home city, Chicago, as I write the closing section of the final chapter of this book. 'World Music Festival, Chicago 2001' has been underway for only two days, but the entire city has, for the third year, been transformed into a stage for world music. Looking at the events scheduled for today – a total of seventeen appear in the official programme – we get some idea of what we might understand 'a stage for world music' really to be.

The metropolis becomes a metaphor for the world, mapping its music and its music cultures so that anyone and everyone can participate in the encounter. The map of the festival deliberately stretches to all districts of the city, to the 'neighbourhoods', as Chicagoans are accustomed to refer to the parsing of their cultural geography. The venue for each concert is marked by a two-letter neighbourhood address, such as 'HP' for Hyde Park, the neighbourhood where the University of Chicago is located. It is perhaps not by chance that the neighbourhood addresses assume the appearance of the car stickers that ascribe national origin, such as 'GB' or 'PL'. Chicago neighbourhoods are rather famous for claiming national and nationalist allegiance, so much so that most residents of the city know that Pilsen is Mexican and the Northwest Side is Polish. A closer look at the map of the city's world music festival, however, reveals that it does not simply replicate the neighbourhood's ethnic and national identities. Perhaps half of the addresses are not just neighbourhoods reconfigured as stages for world music, but are real stages reconfigured, if I may be deliberately redundant, as stages for world music: the Chicago Symphony Center, for example, will host a performance of the Palestinian *'ud* player, Simon Shaheen, this evening, and Algerian raï star, Khaled, is billed for the 'closing concert' on September 30th at the Riviera Theatre. Neighbourhood 'centres', usually dominated by broad-ranging social and civic services to the neighbourhood, also become stages. Least surprising of all, so do bastions of folk and traditional music, notably the Old Town School of Folk Music, and many sites of transnational culture-brokering in the city, such as Borders Books and Music.

Were one so inclined, it would be easy enough to dismiss the 'World Music Festival, Chicago 2001' as no more than entertainment and tourism. There is a fair number of well-known worldbeat ensembles, most of them performing at the expensive venues. The festival's organizers, the Mayor's Office of Special Events, makes no bones about the potential to draw tourists to the city as autumn begins, after the summer season of music festivals concentrated in centrally-located Grant Park. The Blues Festival, Jazz Festival, Gospel Festival, Celtic Festival, and Viva Latina, which together punctuated the summer months, have proved that world music brings money to the city, even though they themselves require no admission charge. The concern about attracting culture tourists to Chicago is all the more critical during the 'World Music Festival, Chicago 2001' because of the uncertainty accompanying the shock of the attacks on September 11th.

It is also the case that anyone wishing to attack world music as homogenized global pop, cultural imperialism made sonorous, would find convenient targets. Such attacks, however, would misinterpret the ways in which world music had remapped the city and responded to an enormous range of local factors. The densest neighbourhood cartography, for example, is that provided by blues musicians. It is dense because the map of the festival merely draws attention to what is already a dense, cosmopolitan music culture, known throughout the world as 'Chicago blues' or 'urban blues'. In contrast, the weekend providing the world music encounters for this closing section is filled with Native American events, the dominant of which is the Eschikagou Indian Powwow. So complex are the contexts for this final great gathering of the powwow season, which begins in the western American states and Canadian provinces, and moves across the continent to conclude in Chicago, that it is almost impossible to sort them out. The performances

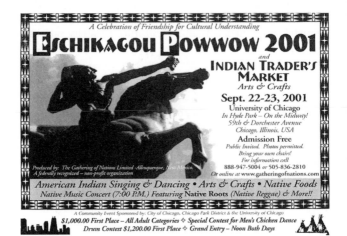

10. Postcard advertising the Eschikagou Powwow 2001, featuring the Native American horseman from the monument at the entrance to Grant Park at the intersection of Michigan Avenue and the Congress Parkway

World Music

begin with a 'Native American Equinox Celebration', which, indeed, takes place today, the vernal equinox. The powwow itself, historically an indigenization of identity and resistance among the peoples of the Great Plains, will occupy the site initially located on the map of Chicago at the World's Columbian Exposition of 1893, the fairgrounds where the first ethnographic recordings of world music were made. A visible, highly promoted set of weekend performances, the Eschikagou Indian Powwow responds to the ideological struggle for identity in 21st-century North America by historicizing through musical performance the unchecked encounter that pushed Native Americans from the very lands across which their 2001 powwow season has moved.

Is the festival of world music just another instance of unchecked globalization and the victimization of indigenous and local musicians to buttress the power of the producers of worldbeat? Only if one wishes to treat it monolithically, as a single event that is no more nor less than a metaphor for the hegemony of the West. And throughout this book I have resisted doing precisely that. A festival is not a single, concentrated moment for the performance of world music. It results, rather, from the confluence of many different histories. The historical scaffolding that gives structure to the world music festival comprises at least three different levels. On the first level, musicians and audiences continue to respond, the festival notwithstanding, to local ethnic, national, and religious communities. Music-making at this level intersects with other events at the festival and thus establishes connections beyond the local themes. The music itself dominates the stage. The spotlight is focused on jazz or Afro-Cuban fusion or Celtic dance music or raï. It might also be the case that a holiday or historical event is celebrated, effectively reconnecting the music to context through revival, which depends on festivals for its lifeblood. Finally, there can be no doubt that world music festivals explicitly attempt to reconfigure music itself as a means of remapping the world without boundaries, thereby charting a utopian world in which local, ethnic, racial, and religious difference dissolve. In that utopian world the encounter with world music is denied to no one.

In the ethnographic present of this closing section the festival of world music is as ubiquitous as it is everyday. No reader of this book need look very far nor wait very long before having the opportunity to attend such a festival. Though I have made a case for the festivalization of world music at the turn of our century, I want to caution the reader from regarding that festivalization as the teleological endpoint of an historical *longue durée* for world music. The types of encounter brought about by a world music festival are not new, and they are surely not the inevitable convergence of historical trends in the new millennium. Some forms of encounter have disappeared, but others have increased in number and variety. There is little – I should argue, no – evidence that the abundant ways of encountering world music today show any signs of abating. If we examine the encounters that fill a world music festival today more ethnographically, as ethnomusicologists but also as global citizens in the 21st century, we recognize that each event, placed on the stage of a metropolis remapped as the world, bears witness to a different kind of encounter. It may or may not require our participation, and it may or may not alter the ways we interact as selves and others. The history of encounter from which world music has emerged, however, is not about to come to a halt. Each of us – ethnomusicologist, musician, avid amateur, passive listener – will increasingly encounter the music of the world in a growing variety of ways, drawing us ineluctably into a world, the identity and culture of which is no longer separable from our own lives.

References

Here are the details of the works and researches discussed in this book. Since the early 1990s, it has become common practice to publish CDs with books on world music, especially when the book has grown from extensive fieldwork. In the lists that follow, therefore, I have indicated when a book includes a CD.

Preface

Charles Keil and Steven Feld, *Music Grooves: Essays and Dialogues* (University of Chicago Press, 1994)

Bruno Nettl, *The Western Impact on World Music: Change, Adaptation, and Survival* (Schirmer Books, 1985)

Bruno Nettl *et al.*, *Excursions in World Music*, 3rd edn. (Prentice Hall, 2001)

Timothy D. Taylor, *Global Pop: World Music, World Markets* (Routledge, 1997)

Jeff Titon *et al.*, *Worlds of Music*, 3rd edn. (Schirmer Books, 1992)

Chapter 1

David W. Ames and Anthony V. King, *Glossary of Hausa Music and Its Social Contexts* (Northwestern University Press, 1971)

Pi-yen Chen, *Chants of the Chinese Buddhist Monasteries* (A-R Editions, forthcoming) (CD included)

Stephen Greenblatt, *Marvelous Possessions: The Wonder of the New World* (Oxford University Press, 1991)

Jean de Léry, *History of a Voyage to the Land of Brazil, Otherwise Called America*, tr. Janet Whatley (University of California Press, 1999)

Charles Seeger, *Studies in Musicology, 1935–1975* (University of California Press, 1977)

Charles Seeger, *Studies in Musicology II, 1929–1979*, ed. Ann M. Pescatello (University of California Press, 1994)

Lawrence E. Sullivan (ed.), *Enchanting Powers: Music in the World's Religions* (Harvard University Center for the Study of World Religions, 1997)

Deborah Wong, *Sounding the Center: History and Aesthetics in Thai Buddhist Performance* (University of Chicago Press, 2001) (CD included)

Chapter 2

Roger D. Abrahams and John F. Szwed (eds.), *After Africa: Extracts from British Travel Accounts and Journals of the Seventeenth, Eighteenth, and Nineteenth Centuries Concerning the Slaves, Their Manners, and Customs in the British West Indies* (Yale University Press, 1983)

Gregory F. Barz and Timothy J. Cooley (eds.), *Shadows in the Field: New Perspectives for Fieldwork in Ethnomusicology* (Oxford University Press, 1997)

Emmanuel Chukwudi Eze (ed.), *Race and the Enlightenment: A Reader* (Blackwell, 1997)

Johann Gottfried Herder, *Abhandlung über den Ursprung der Sprache* (Christian Friedrich Voβ, 1770)

Johann Gottfried Herder, '*Stimmen der Völker in Liedern*' and *Volkslieder*, 2 vols (Weygandsche Buchhandlung, 1778–9)

Louis Pinck, *Verklingende Weisen: Lothringer Volkslieder*, 5 vols (Lothringer Verlags- und Hilfsverein *et al.*).

Chapter 3

Virginia Danielson, *The Voice of Egypt: Umm Kulthum, Arabic Song, and Egyptian Society in the Twentieth Century* (University of Chicago Press, 1997)

Ruth Davis, *A Musical Ethnography of Palestine, 1936–1937* (A-R Editions, forthcoming)

Robert Lachmann, *Jewish Cantillation and Song in the Isle of Djerba* (Archives of Oriental Music, The Hebrew University, 1940)

Ali Jihad Racy, 'Historical Worldviews of Early Ethnomusicologists', in *Ethnomusicology and Modern Music History*, ed. Stephen Blum, Philip V. Bohlman, and Daniel M. Neuman (University of Illinois Press, 1990), pp. 68–91

Marc Schade-Poulsen, *Men and Popular Music in Algeria: The Social Significance of Raï* (University of Texas Press, 1999)

Guillaume-André Villoteau, 'De l'état actuel de l'art musical en Egypte', in *Description de l'Egypte*, 2nd edn. (C. L. F. Panckoucke, 1826)

Edward Said, *Orientalism* (Random House, 1978)

Chapter 4

Moses Asch and Alan Lomax (eds.), *The Leadbelly Songbook: The Ballads, Blues and Folksongs of Huddie Ledbetter* (Oak Publications, 1962)

Philip V. Bohlman and Otto Holzapfel, *The Folk Songs of Ashkenaz* (A-R Editions, 2001)

S. M. Ginsburg and P. S. Marek, *Evreiskie narodnye pesni v Rossii* [Jewish Folk Songs from Russia] (Voskhod, 1901)

Johann Gottfried Herder, '*Stimmen der Völker in Liedern*' and *Volkslieder*, 2 vols (Weygandsche Buchhandlung, 1778–9)

Franz Liszt, *The Gypsy in Music*, tr. Edwin Evans (William Reeves, 1859)

Alan Lomax, *Folk Song Style and Culture* (American Association for the Advancement of Science, 1977)

Alan Lomax, *Hard Hitting Songs for Hard-Hit People* (Oak Publications, 1967)

John A. Lomax, *Cowboy Songs and Other Frontier Ballads* (Sturgis and Walton, 1910)

John A. Lomax and Alan Lomax, *Folk Song: U.S.A., the 111 Best American Ballads*, ed. Charles Seeger and Ruth Crawford Seeger (Duell, Sloan and Pearce, 1947)

John A. Lomax and Alan Lomax, *Negro Folk Songs as Sung by Lead Belly* (Macmillan, 1936)

Chapter 5

Benedict Anderson, *Imagined Communities: Reflections on the Origins and Spread of Nationalism*, 2nd edn. (Verso, 1991)

Malcolm Boyd, 'National Anthems', in *The New Grove Dictionary of Music and Musicians*, 2nd edn. (Macmillan, 2001) vol. 17, pp. 654–87

Paul Gambaccini *et al.*, *The Complete Eurovision Song Contest Companion 1999* (Pavilion, 1999)

Michael Herzfeld, *Cultural Intimacy: Social Poetics in the Nation-State* (Routledge, 1997)

Bruno Nettl, 'Arrows and Circles: An Anniversary Talk about Fifty Years of ICTM and the Study of Traditional Music', *Yearbook for Traditional Music* 30 (1998): 1–11

Paul Nettl, *National Anthems*, 2nd edn. (Frederick Ungar, 1967)

John Philip Sousa, *National, Patriotic and Typical Airs of All Lands* (H. Coleman, 1890)

Chapter 6

Amit Chaudhuri, *Afternoon Raag* (William Heinemann, 1993)

W. E. B. Du Bois, *The Souls of Black Folk*, ed. Henry Louis Gates, Jr (Bantam, 1989)

Paul Gilroy, *The Black Atlantic: Double Consciousness and Modernity* (Harvard University Press, 1993)

A. Z. Idelsohn, *Hebräisch-orientalischer Melodienschatz*, 10 vols (Benjamin Harz *et al.*, 1914–32)

Peter Manuel, *Cassette Culture: Popular Music and Culture in North India* (University of Chicago Press, 1993)

Carol E. Robertson (ed.), *Musical Repercussions of 1492: Encounters in Text and Performance* (Smithsonian Institution Press, 1992)

Martin Stokes (ed.), *Ethnicity, Identity and Place: The Musical Construction of Place* (Berg, 1994)

Chapter 7

Walter Benjamin, *The Arcades Project*, tr. Howard Eiland and Kevin McLaughlin (Harvard University Press, 1999)

Daphne Berdahl, Matti Bunzl, and Martha Lampland (eds.), *Altering States: Ethnographies of Transition in Eastern Europe and the Former Soviet Union* (University of Michigan Press, 2000)

Simon Broughton, Mark Ellingham, and Richard Trillo, *World Music*, vol. 1: *Africa, Europe and the Middle East* (The Rough Guides, 1999)

Simon Broughton and Mark Ellingham (eds.), *World Music*, vol. 2: *Latin and North America, Caribbean, India, Asia and Pacific* (The Rough Guides, 2000)

Manu Dibango, *Three Kilos of Coffee: An Autobiography*, tr. Beth G. Raps (University of Chicago Press, 1994)

Mark Slobin (ed.), *Retuning Culture: Musical Change in Central and Eastern Europe* (Duke University Press, 1996)

Further reading

The following suggestions are intended as a starting point for the reader wishing to explore further the themes discussed in each of the chapters of this book.

Chapter 1

Nicholas Cook and Mark Everist (eds.), *Rethinking Music* (Oxford University Press, 1999)

Zoila S. Mendoza, *Shaping Society through Dance: Mestizo Ritual Performance in the Peruvian Andes* (University of Chicago Press, 2000)

Regula Burckhardt Qureshi, *Sufi Music of India and Pakistan: Sound, Context and Meaning in Qawwali* (University of Chicago Press, 1995) (CD included)

Lewis Rowell, *Music and Musical Thought in Early India* (University of Chicago Press, 1992)

Martin Stokes, *The Arabesk Debate: Music and Musicians in Modern Turkey* (Oxford University Press, 1992)

Bell Yung and Helen Rees (eds.), *Understanding Charles Seeger, Pioneer in American Musicology* (University of Illinois Press, 1999)

Chapter 2

Philip V. Bohlman, *Herder on Music and Nationalism* (University of California Press, forthcoming)

Georgina Born and Dave Hesmondhalgh (eds.), *Western Music and Its*

Others: Difference, Representation, and Appropriation in Music
(University of California Press, 2000)

Erika Brady, *A Spiral Way: How the Phonograph Changed Ethnography*
(University Press of Mississippi, 1999)

Sebastian Klotz (ed.), *Vom tönenden Wirbel menschlichen Tuns: Erich
M. von Hornbostel als Gestaltpsychologe, Archivar und
Musikwissenschaftler* (Schibri-Verlag, 1998)

Thomas O'Neil, *The Grammys: For the Record* (Penguin, 1993)

Klaus P. Wachsmann, *et al.* (eds. and tr.), *Hornbostel Opera Omnia*
(Martinus Nijhoff, 1975)

Chapter 3

Congress of Cairo, *Musique Arabe: le Congrès du Caire de 1932* (CEDEJ,
1992)

Congress of Cairo, *Recueil des travaux du Congrès de Musique Arabe*
(Imprimerie nationale, Boulac, 1934)

Ibn Khaldun, *The Muqaddimah: An Introduction to History*, tr. Franz
Rosenthal, 3 vols (Pantheon, 1958)

Kristina Nelson, *The Art of Reciting the Qur'an* (University of Texas
Press, 1985)

Marie Virolle-Souibès, *La chanson raï* (Karthala, 1995)

Chapter 4

Béla Bartók, *Hungarian Folk Music*, tr. M. C. Calvacoressi (Oxford
University Press, 1931)

Philip V. Bohlman, *Herder on Music and Nationalism* (University of
California Press, forthcoming)

Malcolm Chapman, *The Celts: The Construction of a Myth*
(Macmillan, 1992)

Victor Greene, *A Passion for Polka: Old-Time Music in America*
(University of California Press, 1992)

Charles Keil, Angeliki V. Keil, and Dick Blau, *Polka Happiness* (Temple
University Press, 1992)

John A. Lomax and Alan Lomax, *Negro Folk Songs as Sung by Lead
Belly* (Macmillan, 1936)

Kenny Mathieson (ed.), *Celtic Music* (Backbeat Books, 2001)

Chapter 5

Hermann Kurzke, *Hymnen und Lieder der Deutschen* (Dietrich'sche Verlagsbuchhandlung, 1990)

Gerda Mraz (ed.), *Österreich Ungarn in Lied und Bild* (Christian Brandstätter, 1997)

Irena Paulus, 'Music in Krzysztof Kieslowski's Film *Three Colors: Blue*', *International Review of the Aesthetics and Sociology of Music* 30, 1 (1999): 65–91

R. K. Prahbu (ed.), *Songs of Freedom: An Anthology of National and International Songs from Various Countries of the World* (Popular Prakashan, 1967)

Cris Shore, *Building Europe: The Cultural Politics of European Integration* (Routledge, 2000)

Ted Swedenborg, 'Saida Sultana/Danna International: Transgender Pop and the Polysemiotics of Sex, Nation, and Ethnicity on the Israeli-Egyptian Border', *The Musical Quarterly* 81, 1 (1997): 81–108

Chapter 6

Jocelyne Guilbault, *Zouk: World Music in the West Indies* (University of Chicago Press, 1993)

Dick Hebdige, *Cut 'n' Mix: Culture, Identity, and Caribbean Music* (Routledge, 1987)

Sidney J. Lemelle and Robin D. G. Kelley, *Imagining Home: Class, Culture, and Nationalism in the African Diaspora* (Verso, 1994)

Helen Myers, *Music of Hindu Trinidad: Songs from the India Diaspora* (University of Chicago Press, 1998)

Chapter 7

Robert Cantwell, *Ethnomimesis: Folklife and the Representation of Culture* (University of North Carolina Press, 1993)

Mark DeWitt (ed.), *Music, Travel and Tourism*, special issue of *The World of Music* 41, 3 (1999)

Lita Mathews, *A Powwow Summer across North America* (Gathering of Nations, 2000)

Mark Slobin, *Subcultural Sounds: Micromusics of the West* (University Press of New England, 1993)

Susie J. Tanenbaum, *Underground Harmonies: Music and Politics in the Subways of New York* (Cornell University Press, 1995)

World Music

Listening

These recordings have been selected to give the reader a feel for the artists and genres of music described in each chapter of this book.

Chapter 1

'Festivals of Cusco', vol. 1, *Traditional Music of Peru*, Smithsonian Folkways SF CD 40466

Hesperus, *Spain in the New World: Renaissance, Baroque and Native American Music from New Spain*, Golden Apple GACD 7552 (1990)

Jean Jenkins and Poul Rovsing Olsen (eds.), *Music in the World of Islam*, 6 LPs, Tangent TBX 601 (1976)

Nusrat Fateh Ali Khan, *Qawwali: The Vocal Art of the Sufis* (I), JVC VICG 5029

Nusrat Fateh Ali Khan, *Musst Musst,* Realworld Carol 2314–2 (1990)

Tomás de Torrejón y Velasco, *Maestro Universal del Barroco Hispánico*, Ayuntamiento Villarrobledo M-31109–1994

Chapter 2

Chieftains, *Santiago*, RCA/BMG 09026–68602–2 (1996)

Erich Moritz von Hornbostel (comp.), *The Demonstration Collection of E. M. von Hornbostel and the Berlin Phonogramm-Archiv*, with commentaries by Kurt Reinhard and George List, 2 LPs and accompanying booklet, Ethnic Folkways FE 4175 (1963)

Erich Moritz von Hornbostel (comp.), *Music of the Orient*, 2 LPs and accompanying booklet, Ethnic Folkways FE 4157 (1979, orig. 1934)

Harry Smith (ed.), *Anthology of American Folk Music*, 6 CDs, Smithsonian Folkways 40090/A 28746–A 28751 (1997)

Chapter 3

Absolute Raï, 4 CDs, Virgin France 7243 850 852 2–9

Congrès du Caire, 1932, 2 CDs, Archives Sonores de la Phonothèque Nationale, APN 88/9–10

Umm Kulthūm's recordings are widely available on EMI Egypt and increasingly on remastered CDs

Khaled's CDs are widely available on various labels

Chapter 4

The Celtic Heartbeat Collection, Celtic Heartbeat 82732 (1995)

Leadbelly, *Take This Hammer*, Folkways FA2004

Leadbelly, *Leadbelly Sings Folk Songs*, Folkways FA2488

Alan Lomax (ed.), *World Library of Folk and Primitive Music: The Historic Series*, projected 40 vols, Rounder Records

Muzsikás, *The Bartók Album*, Hannibal HNCD 1439 (1999)

Muzsikás, *The Lost Jewish Music of Transylvania*, Hannibal HNCD 1373 (1993)

Polish-American Dance Music – The Early Recordings: 1927–33, Folklyric Records 9026

Richard K. Spottswood (ed.), *Folk Music in America*, 15 vols, Library of Congress LBC 1–15

Alan Stivell, *Symphonie celtique*, Dreyfus DRYCD-36196 (1995)

Chapter 5

Dana International, *Dana*, IMP Dance 2004 (1993)

Eurovision, Nash' Didan 178 (1998)

Eurovision Song Contest 1956–1999, 2 CDs, Universal 541 347–2 (2000)

Ofra Haza, *Album ha-zahav*, 2 CDs, Hed Arzi Music 15190 (1995)

Zbigniew Preisner, *Bande originale du film Trois Couleurs, Bleu*, Virgin Records America 7243 8 39027 2 9 (1993)

Sürpriz, *Reise nach Jerusalem/Kudüs'e seyahat/Journey to Jerusalem*, BMG 74321 65392 2 (1999)

Swarovski Musik Wattens, *25 europäische Hymnen*, Koch 340 102 F1
(1993)

Unblocked: Music of Eastern Europe, 3 CDs and booklet, Ellipsis Arts
CD 3570–73 (1997)

Chapter 7

Eschikagou Powwow 2000, Gathering of Nations 101 (2001)

Manu Dibango, *Afrijazzy*, Soul Paris/Mélodie (1986)

Manu Dibango, *Homemade*, Mélodie (1987)

Alan Lomax (ed.), *Romania*, vol. 17, *World Library of Folk and
Primitive Music*, Rounder 11661–1759–2 (2001)

Taraf de Haîdouks, *Band of Gypsies*, Nonesuch 79641–2 (2001)

World Music Festival: Chicago 2000, 'Big Chicago Records' BCR 008
(2000)

Index

M

ma 7
Macedonia 129
Maghreb *see* North Africa
magic 5
Mahābhārāta 11, 122
Mama Türk xix, 23, 25
mandola 44
maqām 6, 31, 55
marketing xiv, 19–20, 64
Marley, Bob 118–20
'Marseillaise, La' 100
mediation xi, xvi, 25–6, 50, 60, 63, 68, 87, 123, 127, 141, 144
Mediterranean Sea
  as musical area 50–3, 56, 58–60, 90, 112–13, 124, 133, 138
melograph 16
mestizaje 127
metallophone 117
metaphysics 2, 11, 16, 143
  see also ontology of music
metropolis xvi, 60, 62, 77, 134, 146, 150
Mexico 44, 87, 98, 136
Middle Ages 48, 50, 57
Middle East 53, 98
Middle Passage 35–6, 42, 116
Miller, George xviii
minority
  ethnic 61
  religious 61
missionary 2–3, 14–15, 28, 30, 35, 42, 70, 138
mode 6, 12, 55, 59
Modern Era *see* modernity

modernism 66, 68, 111
modernity xiii, xvi, 21, 37, 48–9, 63, 68, 70, 73, 77, 107, 111–12, 114, 132
Modugno, Domenico 90
Mohammad (the Prophet in Islam) 12, 56
Monaco 98
Montaigne 3
Morocco 34, 47–8, 61, 124
Mountain Chief xix, 23–4, 140
Mozart, Wolfgang 53
multiculturalism xvi, 60, 85, 92, 131, 139
Muqaddimah 51, 57
Music of the Orient (Erich M. von Hornbostel) 27–34
music of the spheres 2, 7
musica mizrakhit 97, 127
musica mundana 7
musical
  as genre of musical theatre 123
musical culture 6, 34, 59, 134, 136, 146–7
musical instruments 2, 5, 7–8, 10–11, 36, 49, 56–9, 61, 63, 80, 116–17, 127, 131–2, 140
musician xvii–xviii, 7, 9–11, 13, 21–2, 32, 34–6, 44, 54, 56, 60–2, 65–6, 75, 78, 80–2, 84–5, 94, 104, 107, 121, 131–5, 137–8, 140, 142, 145, 147, 149–50
mūsīqā 8, 57
mūsīqā al-'arabiyyah 98
mūsīqī 8, 57
Muslim 6, 17–20, 51, 54–5, 57, 59, 62, 92, 98, 111, 126

‹

Expand your collection of
VERY SHORT INTRODUCTIONS

Available now

Visit the
VERY SHORT
INTRODUCTIONS
Web site

www.oup.co.uk/vsi

➤ **Information** about all published titles

➤ News of **forthcoming books**

➤ **Extracts** from the books, including titles
not yet published

➤ **Reviews** and views

➤ **Links** to other **web sites** and main
OUP web page

➤ Information about **VSIs in translation**

➤ **Contact** the editors

➤ **Order** other **VSIs** on-line